Homework Help Science

Ages 10–11
Key Stage 2 / Year 6

Andy Bailey, Jane Harris & Michael Wilkinson

We're the Homework Helpers!

We've thought up lots of fun activities for you!

So grab your pens and pencils...

...and let's get started!

Longman
An imprint of **Pearson Education**

Harlow, England · London · New York · Reading, Massachusetts · San Francisco
Toronto · Don Mills, Ontario · Sydney · Tokyo · Singapore · Hong Kong · Seoul
Taipei · Cape Town · Madrid · Mexico City · Amsterdam · Munich · Paris · Milan

Series editors:
Stuart Wall & Geoff Black
With thanks to Jane Webster for additional material

These people helped us write the book!

A complete range of **Homework Helpers** is available.

		ENGLISH	MATHS	SCIENCE
Key Stage 1	Ages 5–6 Year 1	✓	✓	Science is not included in the National Tests at Key Stage 1
Key Stage 1	Ages 6–7 Year 2	✓	✓	
Key Stage 2	Ages 7–8 Year 3	✓	✓	✓
Key Stage 2	Ages 8–9 Year 4	✓	✓	✓
Key Stage 2	Ages 9–10 Year 5	✓	✓	✓
Key Stage 2	Ages 10–11 Year 6	✓	✓	✓

This tells you about all our other books.

Which ones have you got?

Pearson Education Limited
Edinburgh Gate, Harlow
Essex CM20 2JE, England
and Associated Companies throughout the world

© Pearson Education Limited 2000

The right of Andy Bailey, Jane Harris and Michael Wilkinson to be identified as authors of this work has been asserted in accordance with the Copyright, Designs and Patents Act 1988

All rights reserved; no part of this publication may be reproduced, stored in any retrieval system, or transmitted in any form or by any means, electronic, mechanical, photocopying, recording, or otherwise without either the prior written permission of the Publishers or a licence permitting restricted copying in the United Kingdom issued by the Copyright Licensing Agency Ltd, 90 Tottenham Court Road, London W1P 0LP.

First published 2000

British Library Cataloguing in Publication Data
A catalogue entry for this title is available from the British Library

ISBN 0-582-38157-6

Printed in Great Britain by Ashford Colour Press Ltd, Gosport, Hampshire

This is for grown-ups!

Guidance and advice

Schools are now asked to set regular homework. Government guidelines for Year 6 (ages 10–11) suggest 30 minutes of homework a day. Children are also encouraged to do at least 10–20 minutes of reading.

Experimental and investigative science

The aim of the National Curriculum for science is to develop children's knowledge of scientific ideas, processes and skills, and relate these to everyday experiences. Teachers provide opportunities for children to make predictions, plan experiments, learn how to make their test fair, record results, consider evidence, and then think about their results and the effectiveness of the experiment.

All the activities in this book are written to complement the National Curriculum. The emphasis is on short, enjoyable activities designed to stimulate a child's interest in science. Each activity will take 10–20 minutes, depending on the topic, and the amount of drawing and colouring.

Themes and topics

Throughout the book key words have been set in **bold** text – these highlight the themes and content of the activities, and provide a guide to the topics covered.

Encourage your child

Leave your child to do the activity on their own, but be available to answer any questions. Try using phrases like: That's a good idea! How do you think you could do it? What happens if you do it this way? These will encourage your child to think about how they could answer the question for themselves.

If your child is struggling ...

Children who need help with reading or writing may need you to work with them. If your child is struggling with the writing, ask them to find the answer and then write it in for them. Remember, even if your child gets stuck, be sure to tell them they are doing well.

The activities start on the next page! Have you got your pens and pencils ready?

Check the answers together

When they have done all they can, sit down with them and go through the answers together. Check they have not misunderstood any important part of the activity. If they have, try to show them why they are going wrong. Ask them to explain what they have done, right or wrong, so that you can understand how they are thinking.

You will find answers to the activities at the back of this book. You can remove the last page if you think your child might look at the answers before trying an activity. Sometimes there is no set answer because your child has been asked for their own ideas. Check that your child's answer is appropriate and shows they have understood the question.

Be positive!

If you think your child needs more help with a particular topic try to think of some similar but easier examples. You don't have to stick to the questions in the book – ask your own: Did you like that? Can you think of any more examples? Have a conversation about the activity. Be positive, giving praise for making an effort and understanding the question, not just getting the right answers. Your child should enjoy doing the activities and at the same time discover that learning is fun.

More on Science

There are many activities you can do outside school that will help develop your child's familiarity with science and provide valuable practice. Make sure your child has plenty of experience of weighing, measuring, observing processes and making comparisons. Look for opportunities to help your child practise predicting what will happen, collecting evidence and recording results. The more practice your child gets the more comfortable with science they will become.

Inside a flowering plant

Look carefully at the diagram of a **flowering plant**. Think about the function of each **part**.

Match the letters on the diagram to the descriptions underneath the picture.

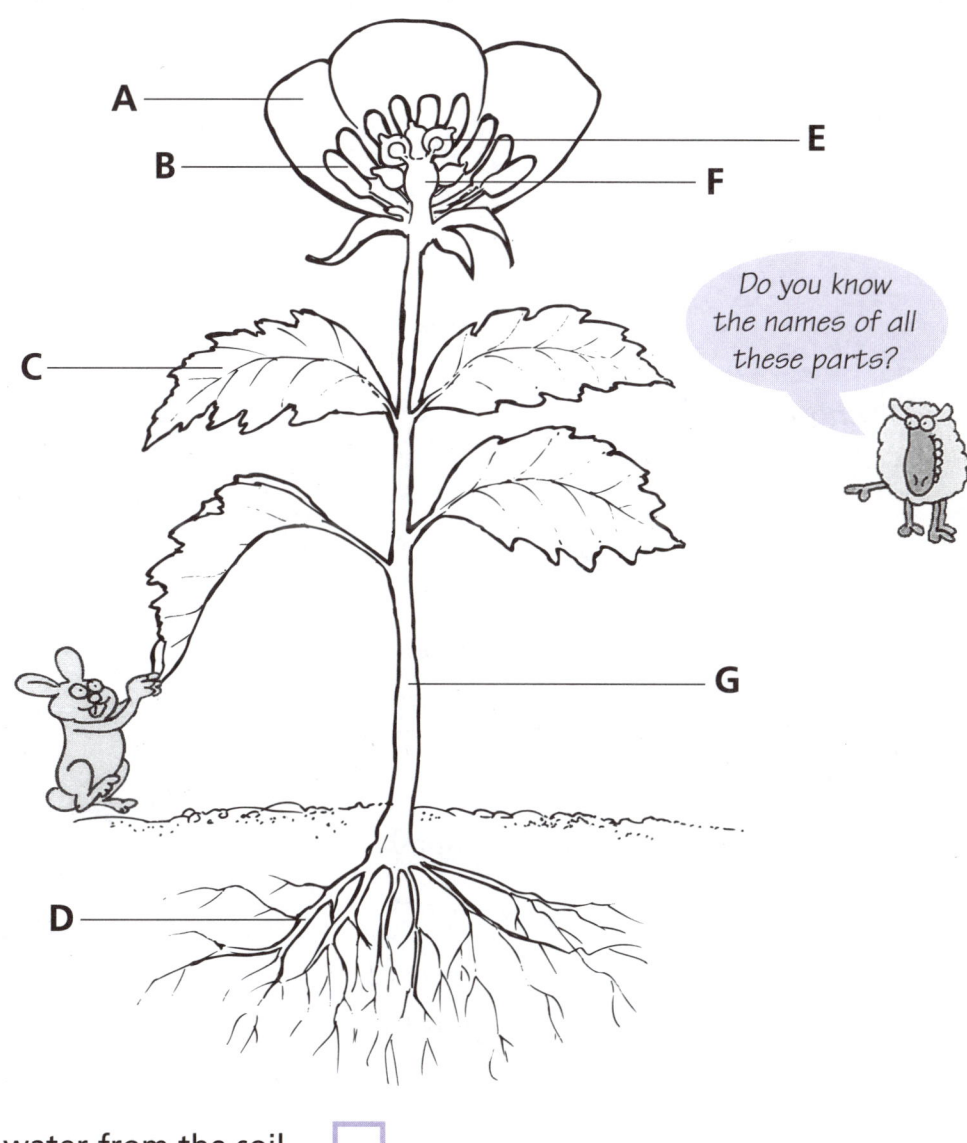

Do you know the names of all these parts?

1   Takes in water from the soil. ☐

2   Makes food for the plant using energy from the sun. ☐

3   Supports the flower and transports nutrients and water to other parts of the plant. ☐

4   Attracts the insects in order for pollination to take place. ☐

5   The male part of the flower containing the pollen. ☐

6   Once pollination takes place seeds grow here. ☐

7   Pollen lands on this and travels down here to the egg cells. ☐

Edible plants

Many plants provide **food** for animals and humans.
We eat all parts of the plant.

1. Look carefully at the foods below. Match them to the parts of the plant that they come from. Write the names in the correct boxes on the opposite page.

- rhubarb
- swede
- tomato
- spinach
- lettuce
- walnuts
- parsnip
- cucumber
- cauliflower
- sunflower seeds
- corn
- apple
- celery
- cabbage
- carrot
- potato
- lemon
- beetroot
- tea
- beans
- peas
- radish
- bean sprouts
- orange
- mango

Petals are rarely eaten.

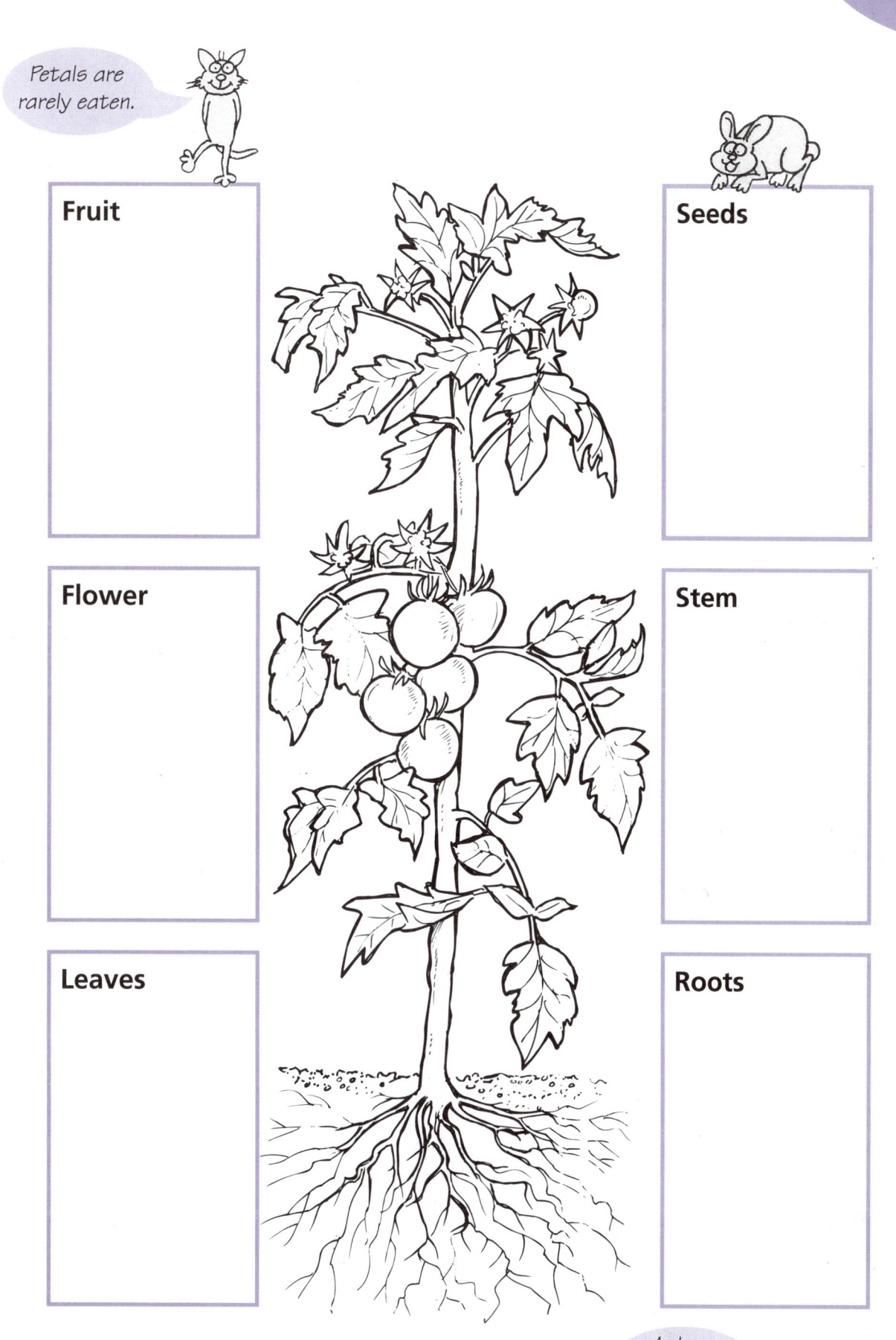

Fruit

Seeds

Flower

Stem

Leaves

Roots

2 Look in the kitchen cupboards at home. How many types of food can you find which come from different parts of plants? Add their names to the correct boxes.

Ask an adult before you look through cupboards.

Growing plants

Class 6 wanted to find out what plants need to grow well, so they have been growing plants for a few weeks. The plants were put in different positions so that they could grow in different conditions.

Class 6 added fertiliser to four of the plants to make sure they had all the nutrients they needed.

Here is a table of Class 6's results.

	Hours of light	Amount of water	Temperature °C	Fertiliser
Plant 1	0 hours	40 cm³	20°C	✓
Plant 2	7 hours	0 cm³	20°C	✓
Plant 3	7 hours	40 cm³	0°C	✓
Plant 4	7 hours	40 cm³	20°C	✗
Plant 5	7 hours	40 cm³	20°C	✓

1 Which plant do you think will grow the best? _____

2 Why? _____
_____

3 Where do you think plant 1 was growing? _____

4 Why? _____
_____

5 Where do you think plant 3 was growing? _____

6 Why? _____
_____

7 Make a list of the conditions that plants need to grow well.

_____   _____

_____   _____

8

8 Look carefully at the pictures of the plants below and see if you can identify which plant was which in Class 6's test.

Write the number of the plant underneath each picture.

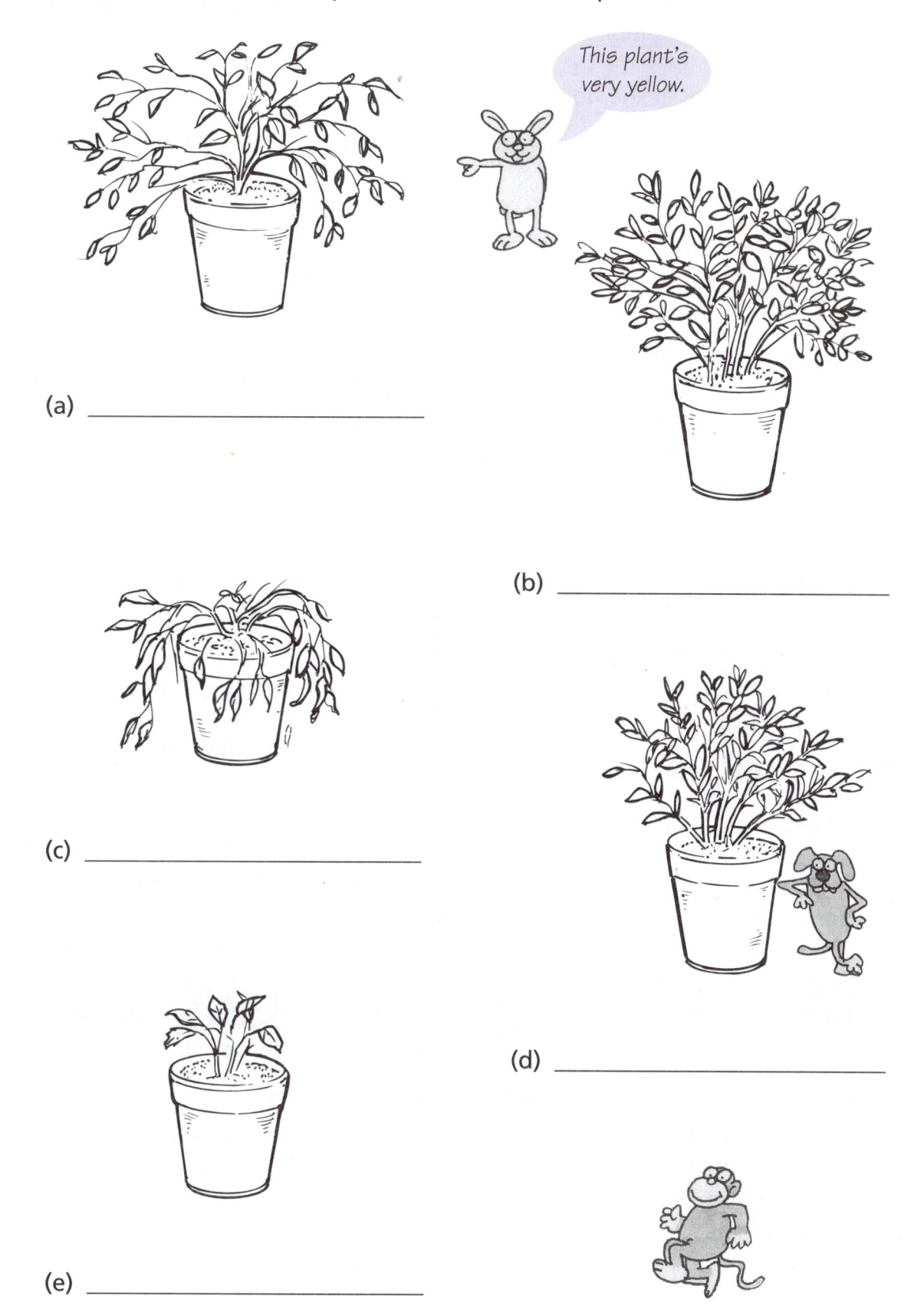

This plant's very yellow.

(a) _____

(b) _____

(c) _____

(d) _____

(e) _____

Green food

Plants are different from other living things because they are able to **make their own food**.

Animals and humans have to get their food from plants or other animals.

Read the sentences in the boxes underneath the picture.

Put the number of each sentence in the correct box on the diagram to show how plants make their food.

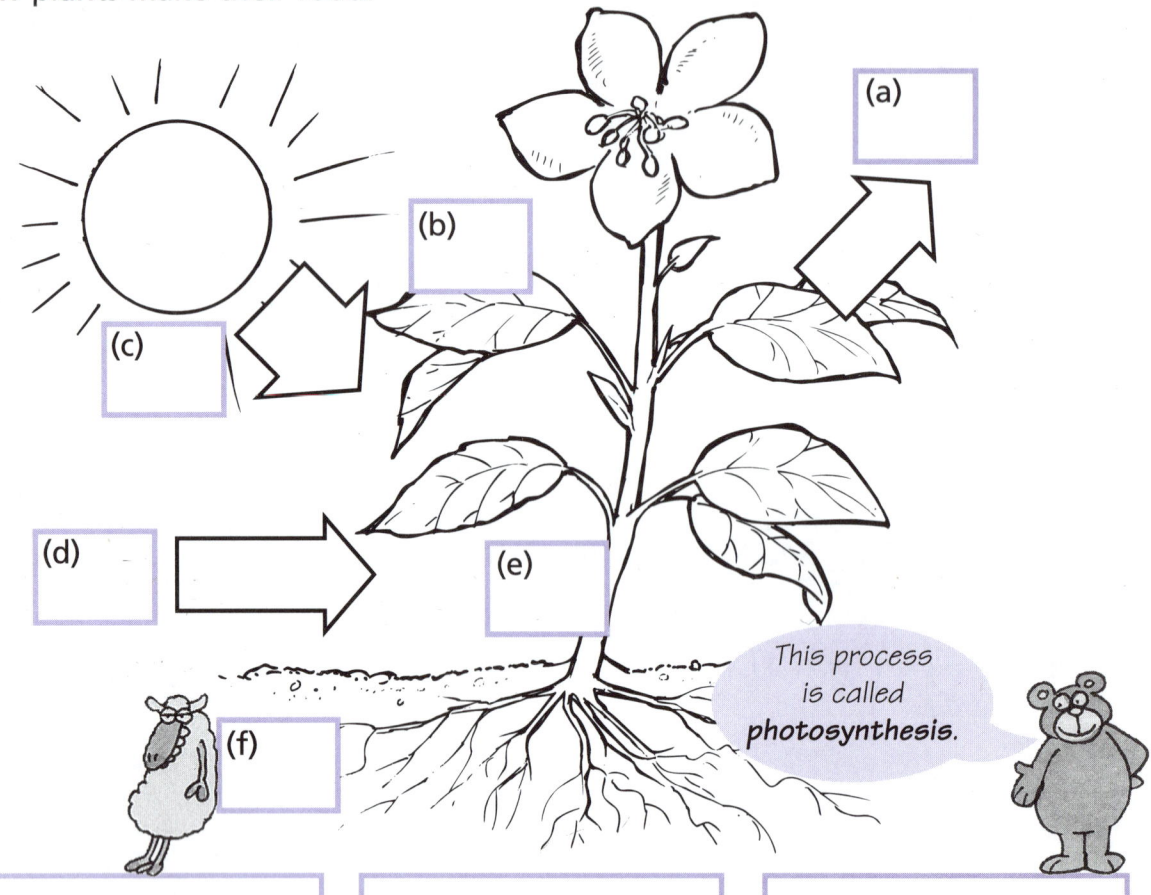

(a)

(b)

(c)

(d)

(e)

(f)

This process is called **photosynthesis**.

1. The sun is the source of **energy** which the plant needs to make its food.

2. Water is taken up from the soil through the roots.

3. Plants make **oxygen** which comes out through holes in the leaf. We breathe in the oxygen.

4. Leaves contain a green-coloured pigment called **chlorophyll**. This traps the sun's energy.

5. **Carbon dioxide** from the air is taken in and is joined together with the water to make sugar which the plant uses for food.

6. Water is carried from the roots through cells in the stem.

Plant keys

Look closely at these **flowers** then use the **key** to name them.

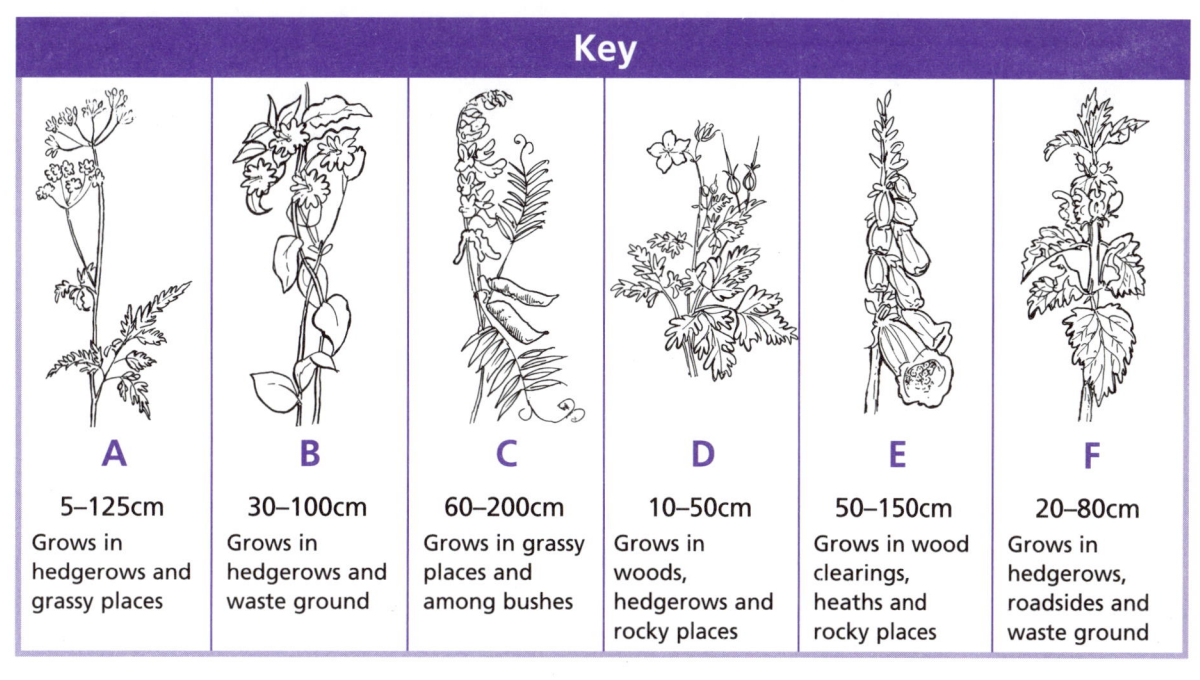

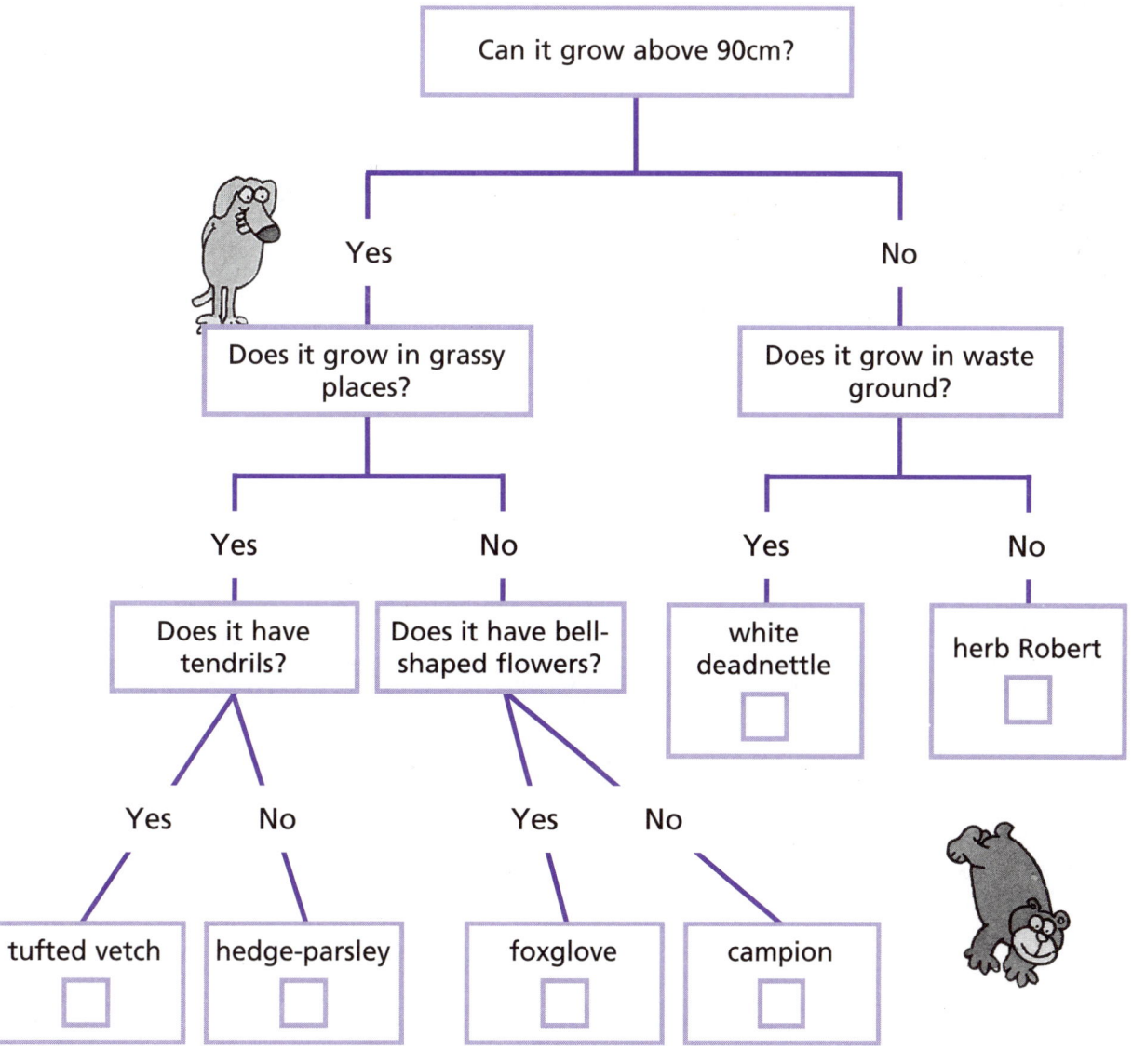

Key

A	B	C	D	E	F
5–125cm	30–100cm	60–200cm	10–50cm	50–150cm	20–80cm
Grows in hedgerows and grassy places	Grows in hedgerows and waste ground	Grows in grassy places and among bushes	Grows in woods, hedgerows and rocky places	Grows in wood clearings, heaths and rocky places	Grows in hedgerows, roadsides and waste ground

Can it grow above 90cm?

- **Yes** → Does it grow in grassy places?
  - **Yes** → Does it have tendrils?
    - **Yes** → tufted vetch
    - **No** → hedge-parsley
  - **No** → Does it have bell-shaped flowers?
    - **Yes** → foxglove
    - **No** → campion
- **No** → Does it grow in waste ground?
  - **Yes** → white deadnettle
  - **No** → herb Robert

Watch the birdie!

Look at the different **habitats** in the illustration.

*A **habitat** is a home for a plant or animal.*

Zone A

Many fish-eating birds perch and nest on cliffs. The sea is full of fish and other animals that provide food for lots of birds.

Zone B

Trees provide seeds, nuts and berries as well as nesting and perching places.

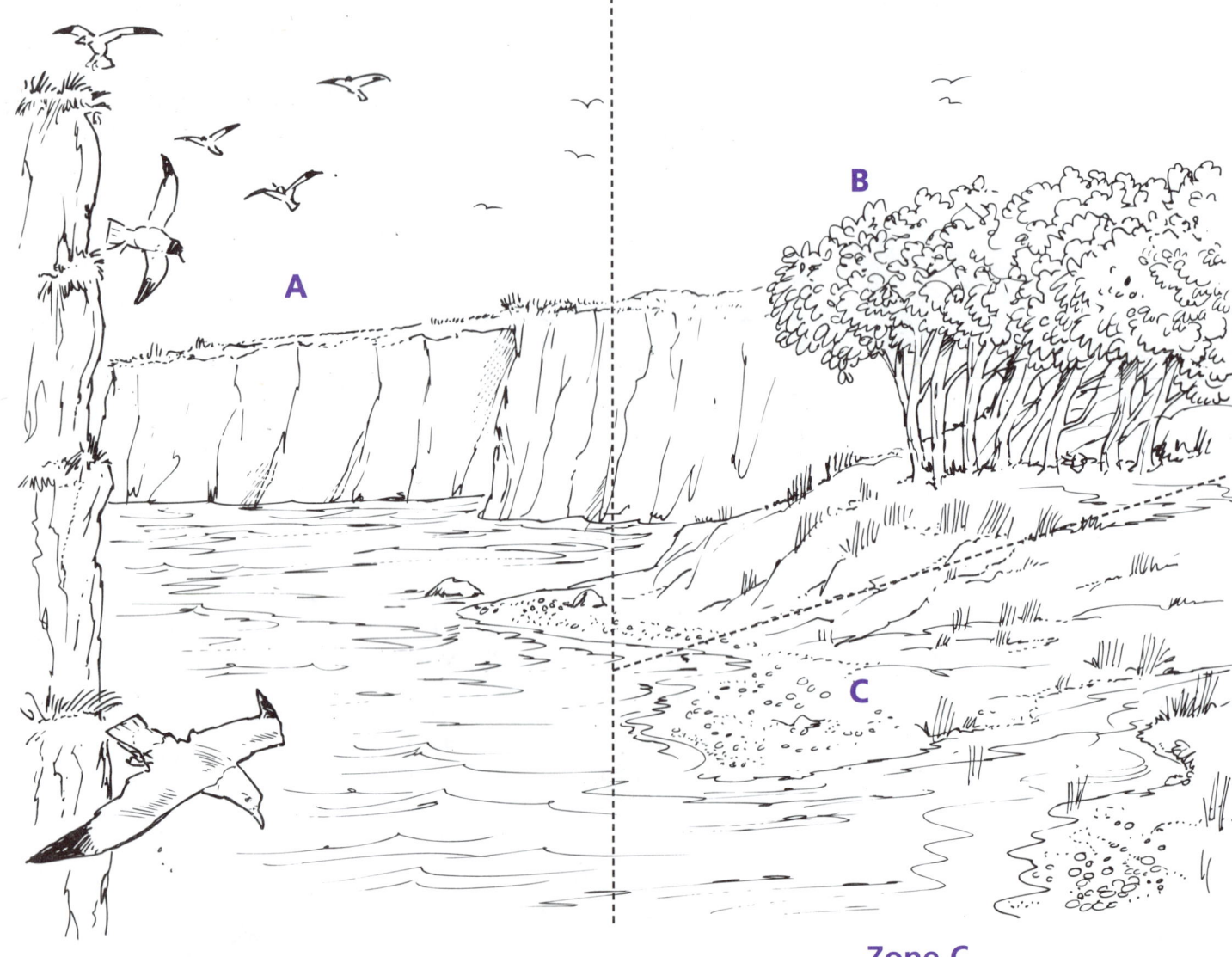

Zone C

Marshes, shallow water and rivers are rich in animals that live in the water and mud.

12

These are **birds** found in each of the habitats.

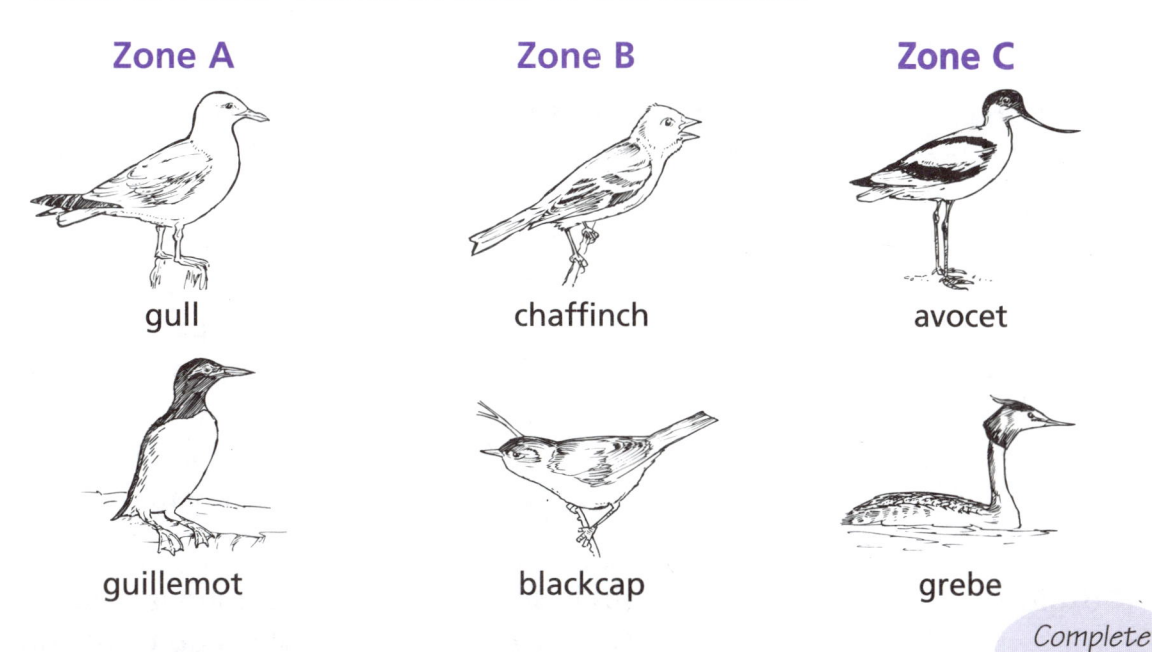

Zone A — gull, guillemot

Zone B — chaffinch, blackcap

Zone C — avocet, grebe

1 Look closely at these birds, particularly their beaks, legs and feet. How are they **adapted** to the habitat in which they live?

Complete the table.

Zone A	Zone B	Zone C

2 Find the names of some more birds that live in each of these zones.

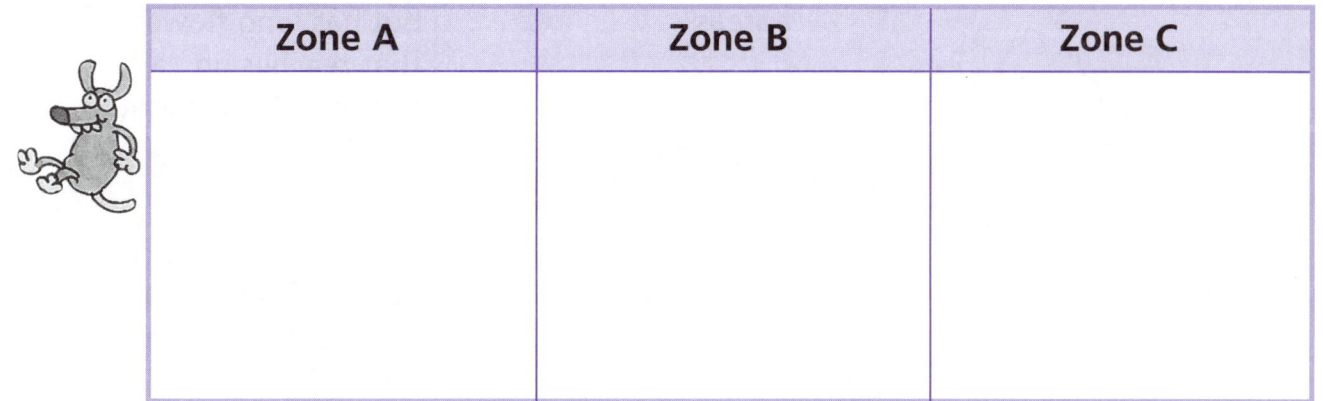

Zone A	Zone B	Zone C

How will you find out about these birds?

Which plant lives there?

Plants are different from one another because each one is **suited** to the **environment** it grows in.

Join up the boxes to show the names of the plants, where they grow and how they are suited to living in those conditions.

The pictures will give you a clue.

Seaweed 	lives in shady areas 	water is stored in the fleshy parts of the plant, and leaves are covered with wax so they don't lose too much water
Foxglove	lives in salty and rocky seashores	has long leaf stalks which go down into the water and the large leaves float on the surface to collect the sunlight
Marram grass	lives in fresh water 	has very long roots so it can reach down to the water
Water lily	lives in desert areas	likes damp conditions but has long flower that reaches up towards the sunlight
Cactus	lives in sandy areas	has gas-filled bubbles to help it float near the surface of the water

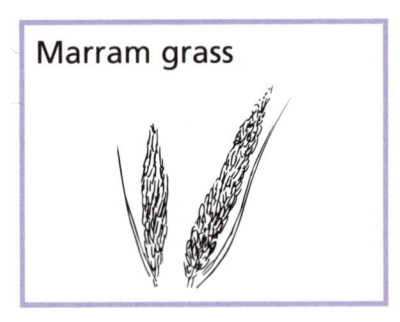

Soils

Sanjay and Emily carried out an investigation on three different types of **soil**.

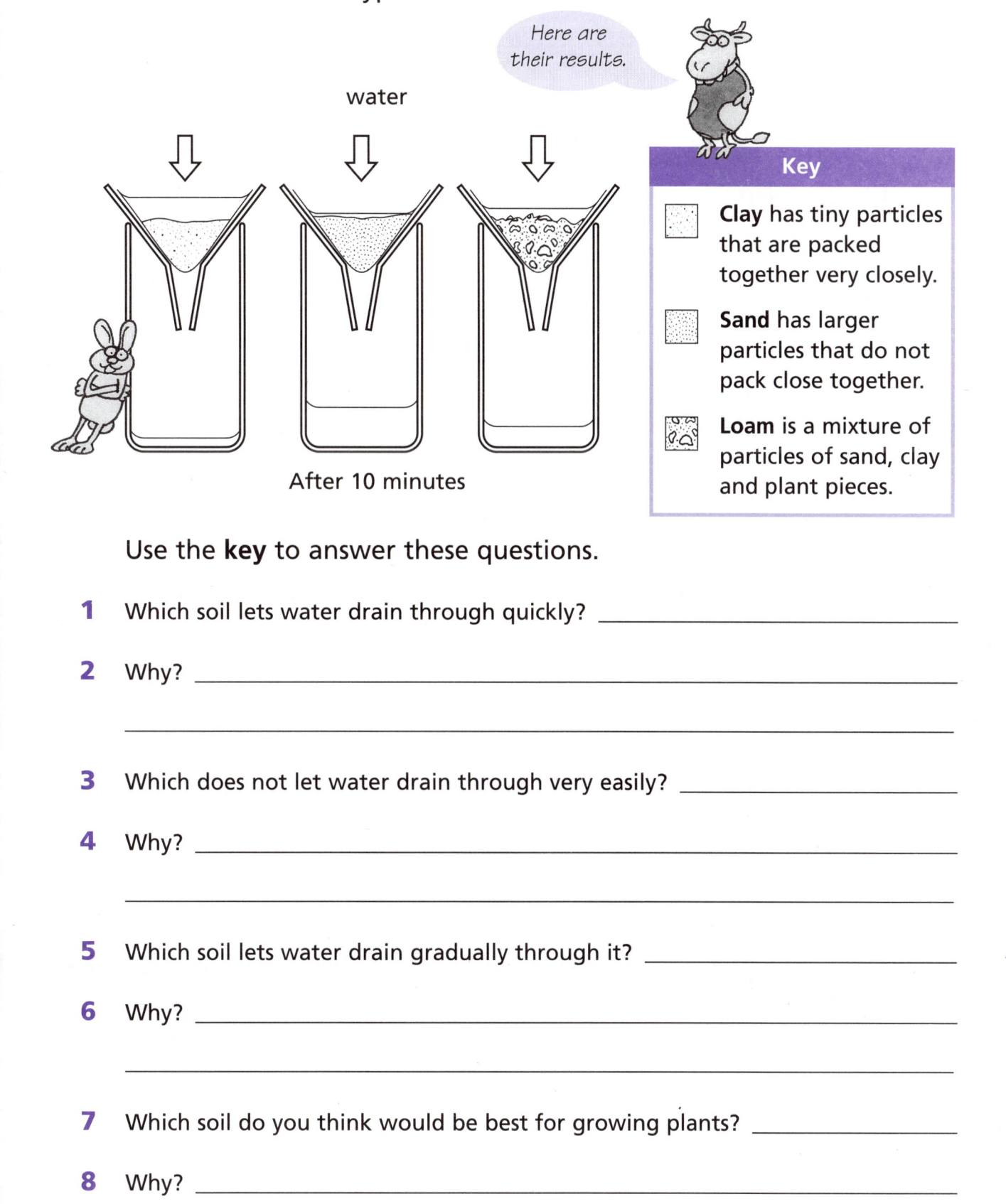

Here are their results.

water

After 10 minutes

Key

Clay has tiny particles that are packed together very closely.

Sand has larger particles that do not pack close together.

Loam is a mixture of particles of sand, clay and plant pieces.

Use the **key** to answer these questions.

1 Which soil lets water drain through quickly? _____

2 Why? _____
_____

3 Which does not let water drain through very easily? _____

4 Why? _____
_____

5 Which soil lets water drain gradually through it? _____

6 Why? _____
_____

7 Which soil do you think would be best for growing plants? _____

8 Why? _____
_____

15

Food chains

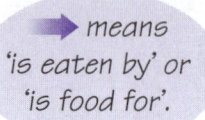

means 'is eaten by' or 'is food for'.

This is a **food chain**.

grass ➡ rabbit ➡ fox

Grass makes its own food. It is called a **producer**. The rabbit eats the grass. The rabbit is called a **consumer**. The fox in turn eats the rabbit. It is also a consumer.

1 Do **consumers** make their own food? Explain your answer.

_____

_____

2 Write this **food chain** in the correct order.

mouse   owl   wheat

_____ ➡ _____ ➡ _____

There are some more food chains here. Write them both out in the correct order.

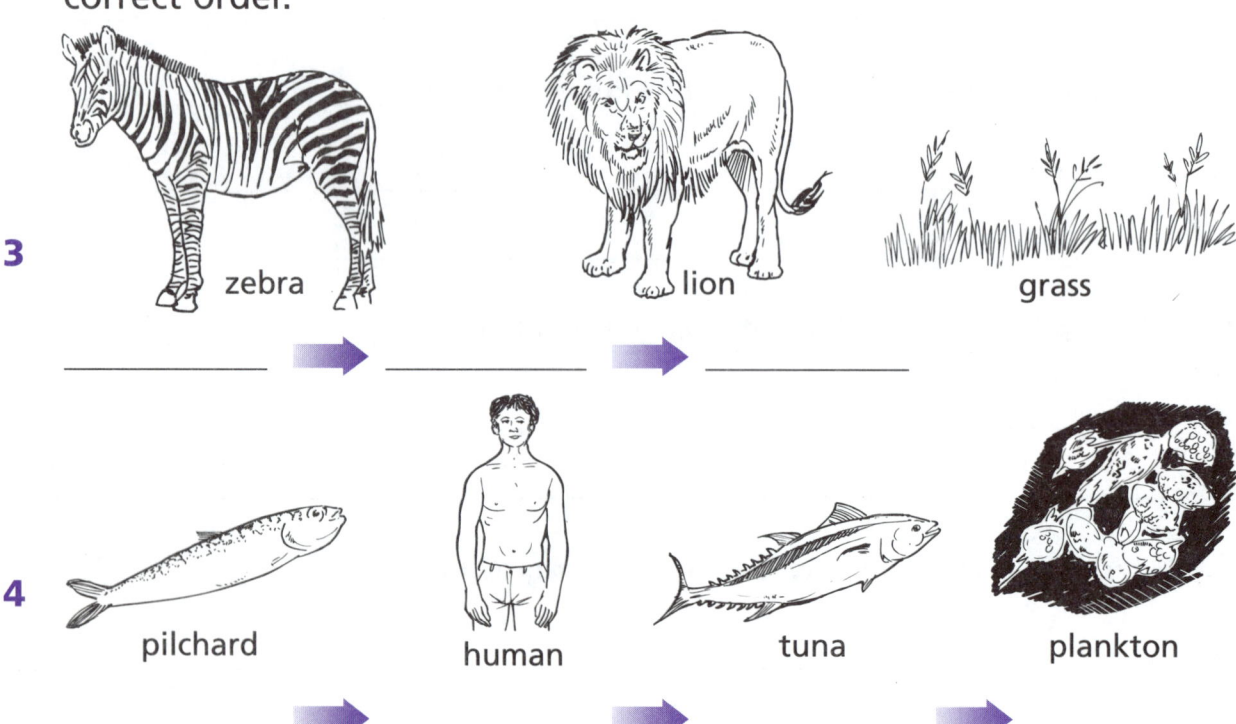

3 zebra   lion   grass

_____ ➡ _____ ➡ _____

4 pilchard   human   tuna   plankton

_____ ➡ _____ ➡ _____ ➡ _____

Write down the correct order.

5 seaweed ➡ winkle ➡ crab ➡ seagull

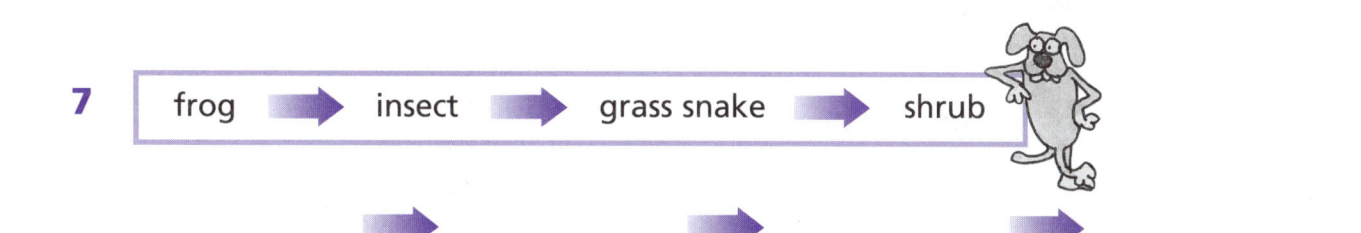

_____ ➡ _____ ➡ _____ ➡ _____

6 caterpillar ➡ leaf ➡ hawk ➡ robin

_____ ➡ _____ ➡ _____ ➡ _____

7 frog ➡ insect ➡ grass snake ➡ shrub

_____ ➡ _____ ➡ _____ ➡ _____

8 Fill in this table using the names of all the **living things** on these two pages.

Producers	Consumers which eat producers	Consumers which eat consumers

9 Where do the **producers** come in each chain? Why?

_____

_____

_____

Useful microbes

Microbes is another name for micro-organisms.

Micro-organisms can be useful as they break down materials. These micro-organisms are living things.

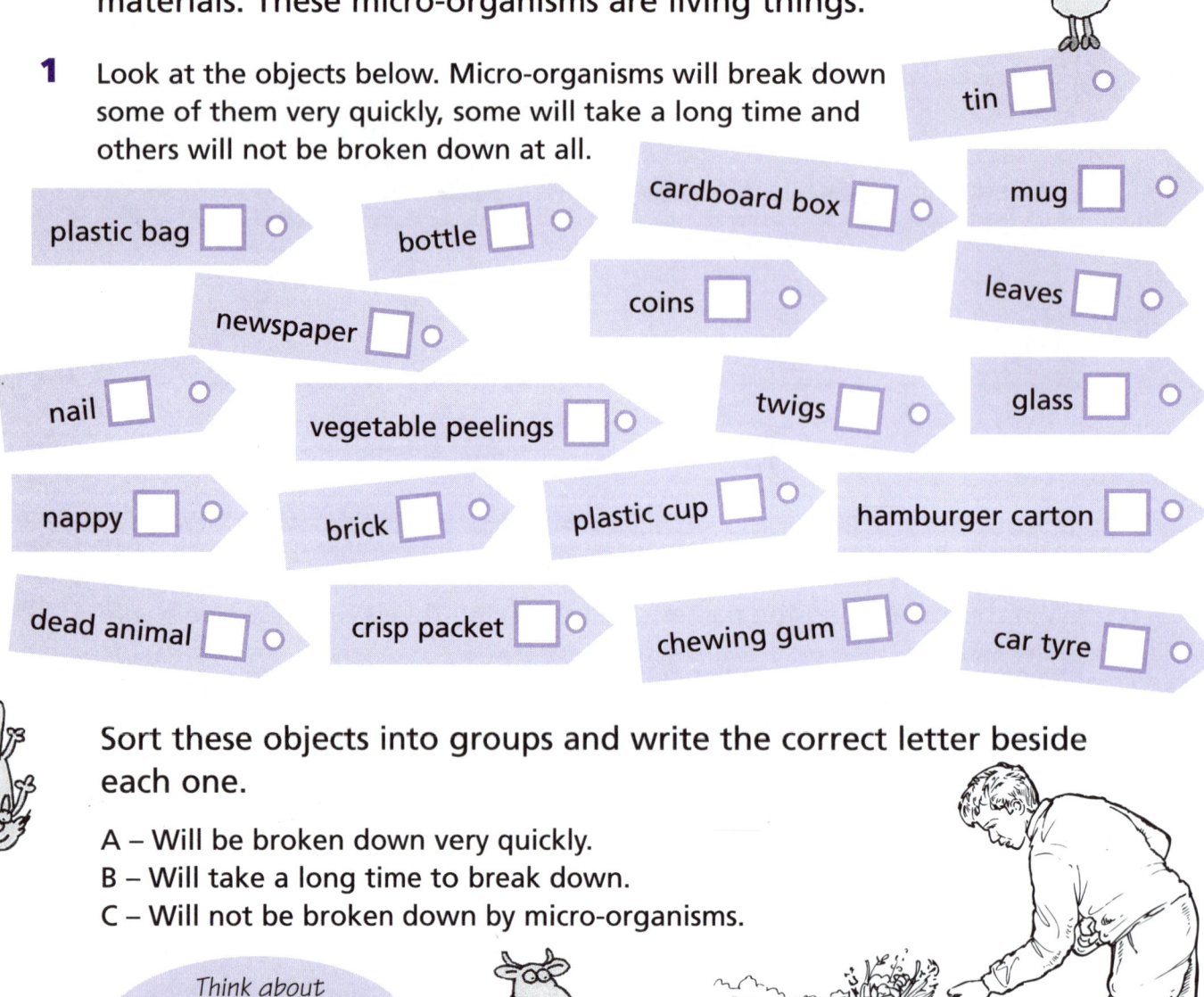

1 Look at the objects below. Micro-organisms will break down some of them very quickly, some will take a long time and others will not be broken down at all.

- plastic bag ☐
- bottle ☐
- cardboard box ☐
- mug ☐
- tin ☐
- newspaper ☐
- coins ☐
- leaves ☐
- nail ☐
- vegetable peelings ☐
- twigs ☐
- glass ☐
- nappy ☐
- brick ☐
- plastic cup ☐
- hamburger carton ☐
- dead animal ☐
- crisp packet ☐
- chewing gum ☐
- car tyre ☐

Sort these objects into groups and write the correct letter beside each one.

A – Will be broken down very quickly.
B – Will take a long time to break down.
C – Will not be broken down by micro-organisms.

Think about things that have been found at historical sights. This will help you.

2 Gardeners have compost heaps to put their garden rubbish in. What happens in there?

_____

_____

3 A lot of the rubbish that is taken away from our houses is buried. Why is it important that we find ways to recycle our rubbish?

_____

_____

Mighty microbes

Micro-organisms are tiny, often too small to be seen, but they can be harmful and can cause disease.

Here is a list of different illnesses.
Some are caused by micro-organisms, and others are not.

1 Look carefully at the list and tick the correct column.

	Caused by micro-organisms	Not caused by micro-organisms
broken arm		
measles		
a cold		
splinter		
nose bleed		
'flu		
bruise		
chicken pox		
bad eyesight		
mumps		
German measles		
stomach bug		
meningitis		

Tick the illnesses that are caused by micro-organisms.

Bacteria and viruses are 'germs'.

2 How do we get these germs?
Put a ring around the causes that are true.

injection from the doctor

washing hands after going to the toilet

putting your hand over your mouth when you cough

sneezing without covering your mouth

letting other people use your handkerchief

19

Clean teeth

Maria has used a disclosing tablet to help show the places where **plaque** has built up on her teeth.
The red dye turns the plaque red.

When she looked in the mirror this is what she saw.

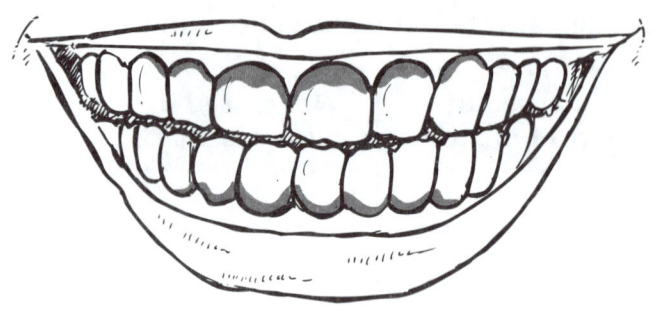

*Micro-organisms live on sugar in your mouth and produce acid. This makes a sticky film called **plaque**.*

1 Where is the plaque?

_____
_____
_____

2 Why do you think it is in these places?

_____
_____

3 How can you get rid of the plaque?

_____
_____

4 If you were Maria's dentist what would you say to her?

_____
_____

Ask an adult if you can try this. You can buy disclosing tablets from chemists.

_____
_____
_____

Growing yeast

Yeast is a micro-organism we use to make bread.
It starts growing when it has sugar to feed on. It gives off a gas when it grows.

Carry out an investigation to see how to make yeast grow more.

You will need

- 4 containers with a small hole at the top
- 4 balloons
- dried yeast
- sugar
- water
- teaspoon

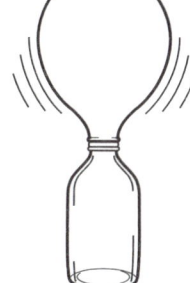

What to do

1. Put some dried yeast into each container.
2. Add some sugar to each container in the following amounts: 3 teaspoons, 2 teaspoons, 1 teaspoon, 0 teaspoons.
3. Add some water and stir. Put the containers in a warm place.
4. Put a balloon over the top of each container so all the gas goes into the balloon. Wait 30 minutes.
5. Measure the size of each balloon and record your results.

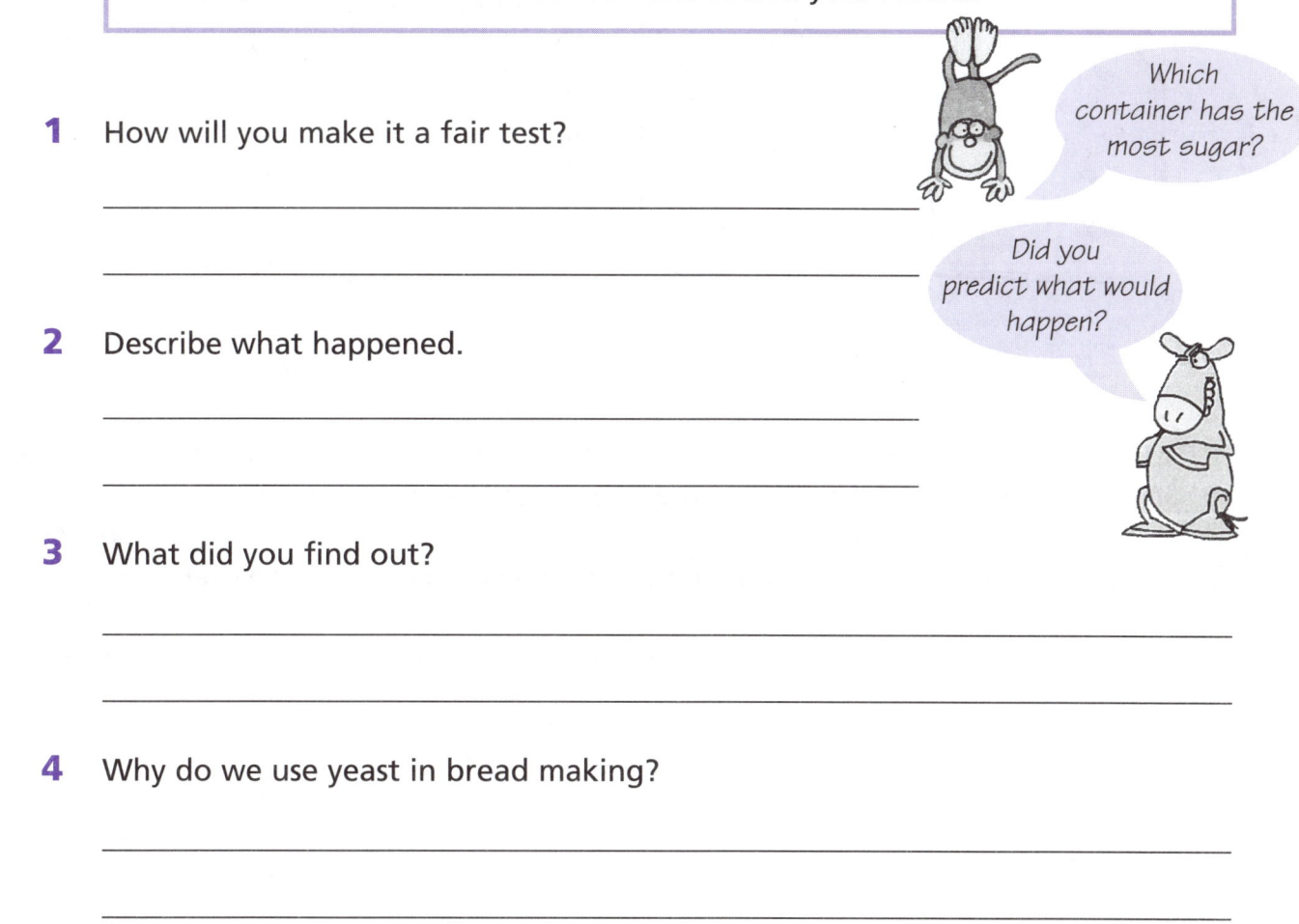

Which container has the most sugar?

Did you predict what would happen?

1. How will you make it a fair test?
   _____
   _____

2. Describe what happened.
   _____
   _____

3. What did you find out?
   _____
   _____

4. Why do we use yeast in bread making?
   _____
   _____

Going mouldy

Lisa and Tom carried out a test to see what caused food to **decay** and whether washing your hands really does make a difference.

They used four slices of bread and did different things to each slice.

Slice 1	they put in a bag with tongs so they didn't touch it.

Slice 2	they put in a bag after wiping the bread with dirty hands.

Slice 3	they put in a bag after washing their hands.

Slice 4	they put in a bag after wiping it over a dirty floor.

They left the sealed bags for a few days. Here are their results.

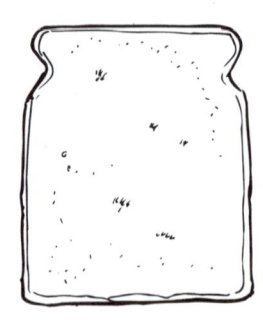

(a) _____ (b) _____ (c) _____ (d) _____

1. Match the picture to the description of what they did with the bread. Write the number of the slice on the line under the correct picture.

2. If you were doing this experiment, how would you make your test fair?

   _____
   _____
   _____
   _____

Preserve it

Micro-organisms need oxygen, water and warmth to survive. They grow best in warm, damp conditions.

This causes a problem when we want to store food. So we have found ways of **preserving** food so the micro-organisms stop growing and the food lasts much longer.

Here are some of the ways of preserving food.

Water is removed from the food so the micro-organisms can't breed. When the food is needed it is placed in water so it can absorb the water and swell up again.

Food is cooled very quickly to a temperature of −18°C. Then it is stored at a temperature of below 0°C. This stops the micro-organisms from breeding.

Food is cooked first to kill all the micro-organisms. Then it is placed in hot cans. The cans are sealed while the food is still hot so no more air can get in.

1 Match the pictures to the correct explanation.

2 Each method of preserving deprives micro-organisms of one of the conditions they need to survive. Fill in the chart below by ticking the appropriate condition for each method of preserving.

Method of preserving	Warmth	Water	Air
freezing			
canning			
drying			

'Deprive' means to stop an object from getting something.

Circuit diagrams

*The objects in a circuit are called **components**.*

Here are some diagrams of electrical **circuits**. For electricity to flow, a circuit must be complete. Look carefully at each circuit to see if the light bulb will light up.

1 Colour in the light bulb yellow if the circuit is complete.

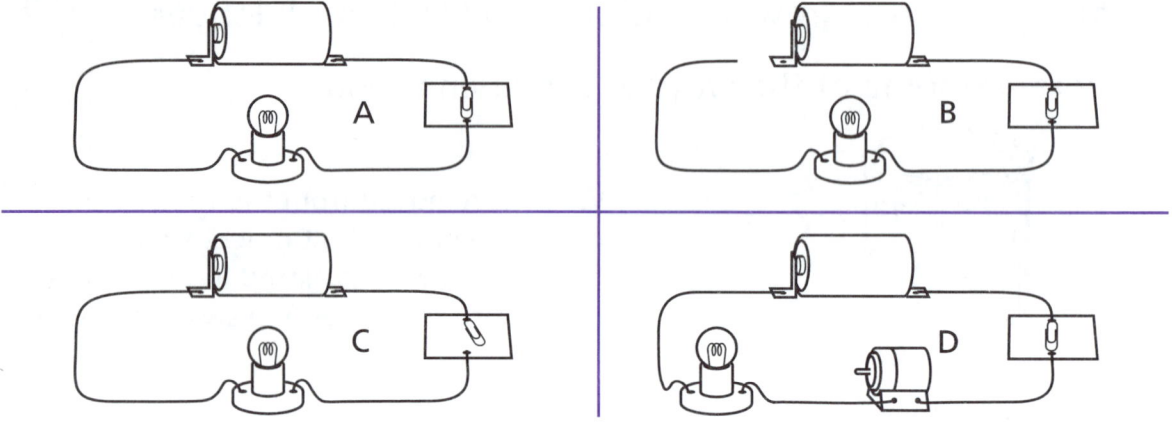

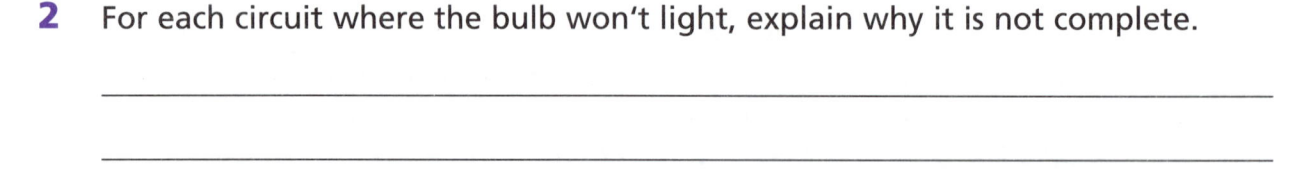

A   B

C   D

2 For each circuit where the bulb won't light, explain why it is not complete.

_____
_____
_____
_____

We can use symbols to draw circuits that are understood by everybody because the same symbol is used everywhere to represent each object.

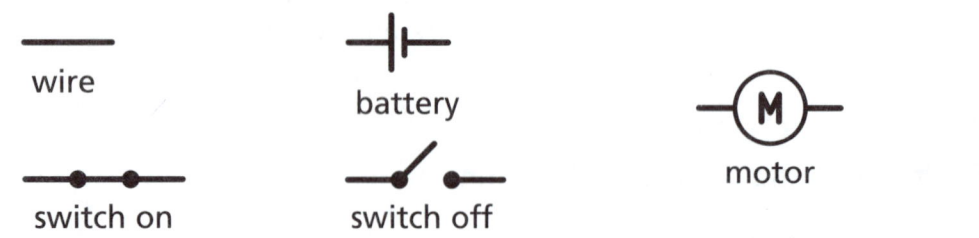

wire

battery

motor

light bulb

switch on

switch off

3 Why do you think it is important that everybody uses the same symbols?

_____
_____

4 Who do you think would need to understand these symbols?

_____
_____

People who make and design circuits are called electrical engineers.

24

5 Look at these circuit diagrams and match them to circuits on the opposite page.

Write the correct letter in each box.

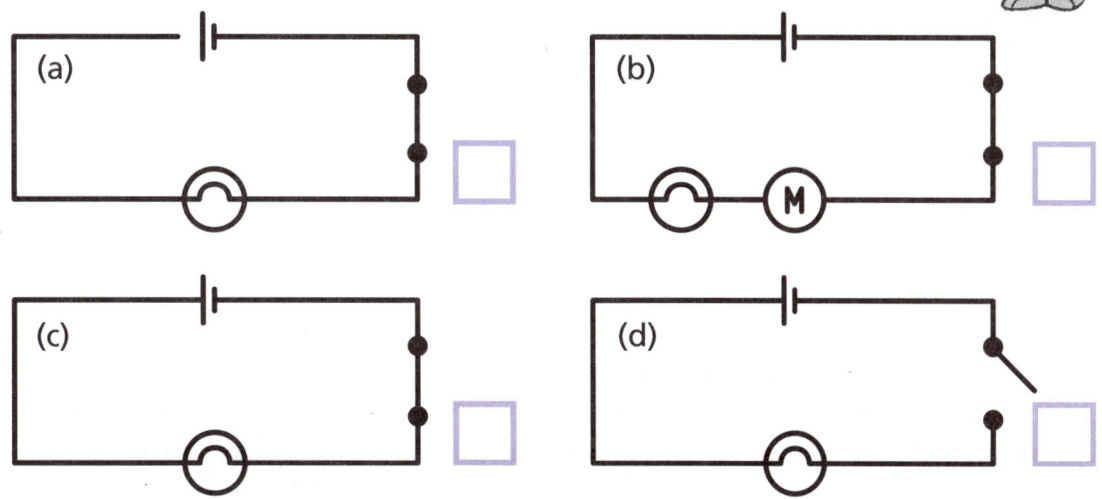

(a)

(b)

(c)

(d)

6 Look at these circuit diagrams. What would you need if you were going to construct the circuits? Fill in the chart.

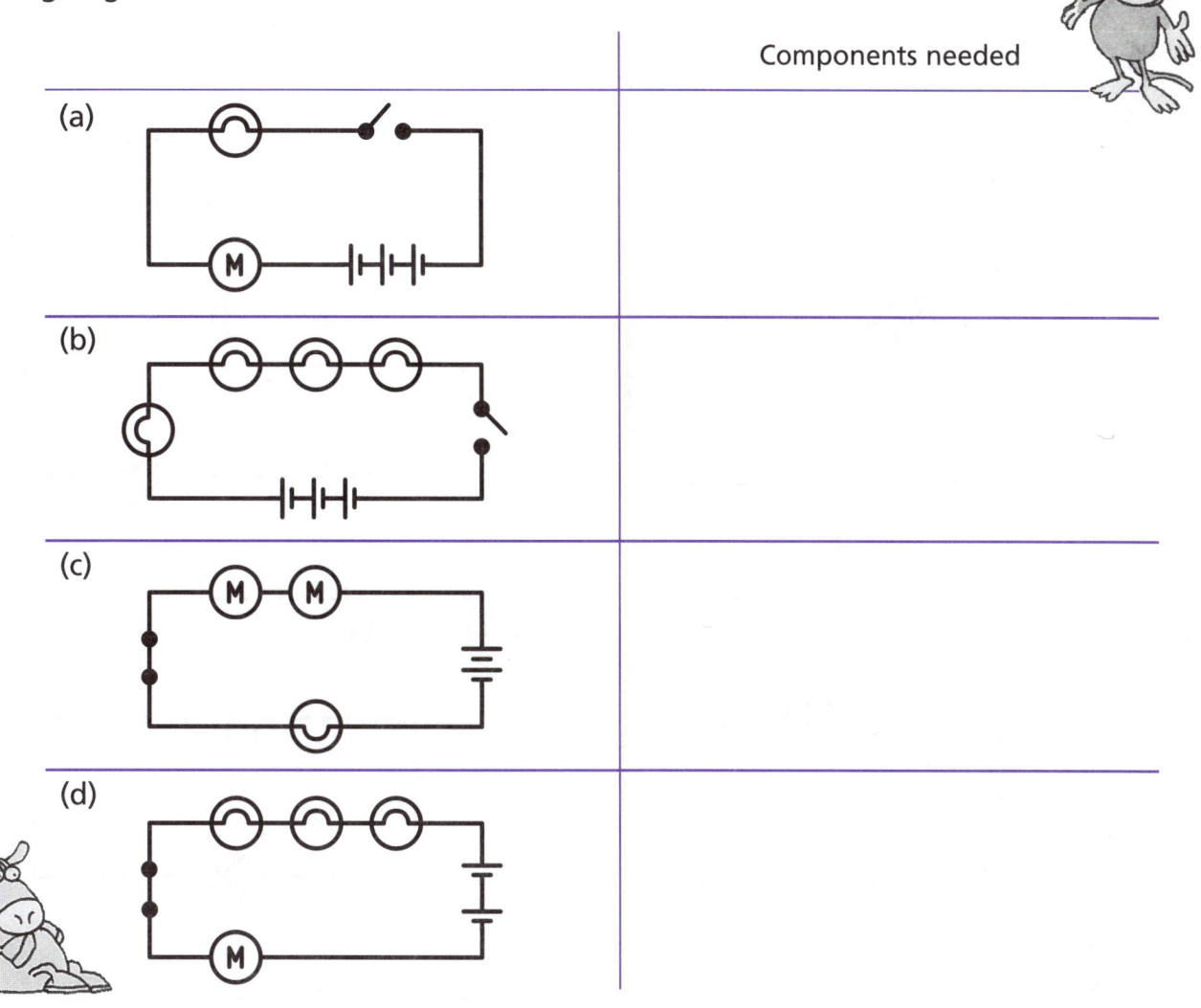

	Components needed
(a)	
(b)	
(c)	
(d)	

25

Bright lights

To make a bulb bright a lot of electricity has to flow through it.

You can make a **bulb** brighter in a number of ways.

1. Look at the list below and put a tick beside the things that would make the bulb brighter.

   fewer bulbs ☐　　　longer wire ☐　　　thicker wire ☐

   adding more bulbs ☐　　　smaller battery ☐

   thinner wire ☐　　　shorter wire ☐　　　bigger battery ☐

2. Look at the pairs of circuit diagrams below. Decide which one of each pair will be the brightest. Explain why it is brighter on the line underneath.

   The more things in a circuit, the less electricity will get to the bulb.

   (a) _____

   This symbol means a coiled wire.

   (b) _____

   (c) _____

Sam and Sara wanted to test for themselves whether the length of the wire in a circuit made a difference to the brightness of the bulb.

Here are their results.

Length of wire	Brightness of bulb
1 m	very bright light
5 m	bright light
10 m	dim light
20 m	very faint light
40 m	no light

3 What can you learn from these results?

_____

_____

_____

4 How did Sam and Sara keep the test fair?

_____

_____

_____

_____

True or false?

5 Look at the statements below. Some are correct, others are wrong. Put a ✓ beside the correct statements. Put a ✗ beside the statements that are wrong.

(a) Electricity will only flow through a complete circuit. ☐

(b) The brightness of a bulb depends on the thickness of the wire. ☐

(c) Most metals are bad conductors. ☐

(d) An electric circuit is a wire joining a switch to a bulb. ☐

Real circuits

There are two ways of connecting bulbs in a circuit.

In a series circuit, the bulbs are next to each other.

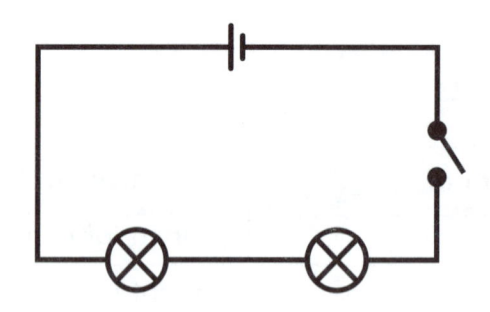

We have found out that if we add more bulbs to the circuit they become dimmer.

This is called a **series circuit**.

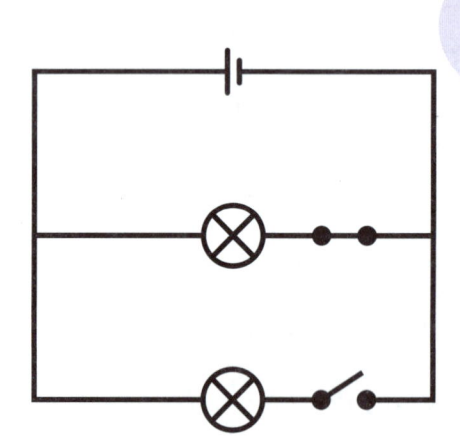

But how do the circuits work in our homes? The lights don't become dimmer when you turn on more lights.

This is called a **parallel circuit**.

1   What will happen to the bulbs if you turn the switch off in the series circuit?
   _____
   Why? _____
   _____

2   What will happen to the bulbs if you turn one switch off in the parallel circuit?
   _____
   Why? _____
   _____

3   Which type of circuit do you think is used in wiring a house?
   _____

Seeing the light

We see objects because light travels from them and enters our eyes.

The objects that give out light are **light sources**. We see other objects because light is **reflected** from a light source and then enters our eyes.

light rays from the candle

1. Look carefully at the pictures below.
   Only one is correct. Put a ✓ beside it and a ✗ beside the ones that are wrong.

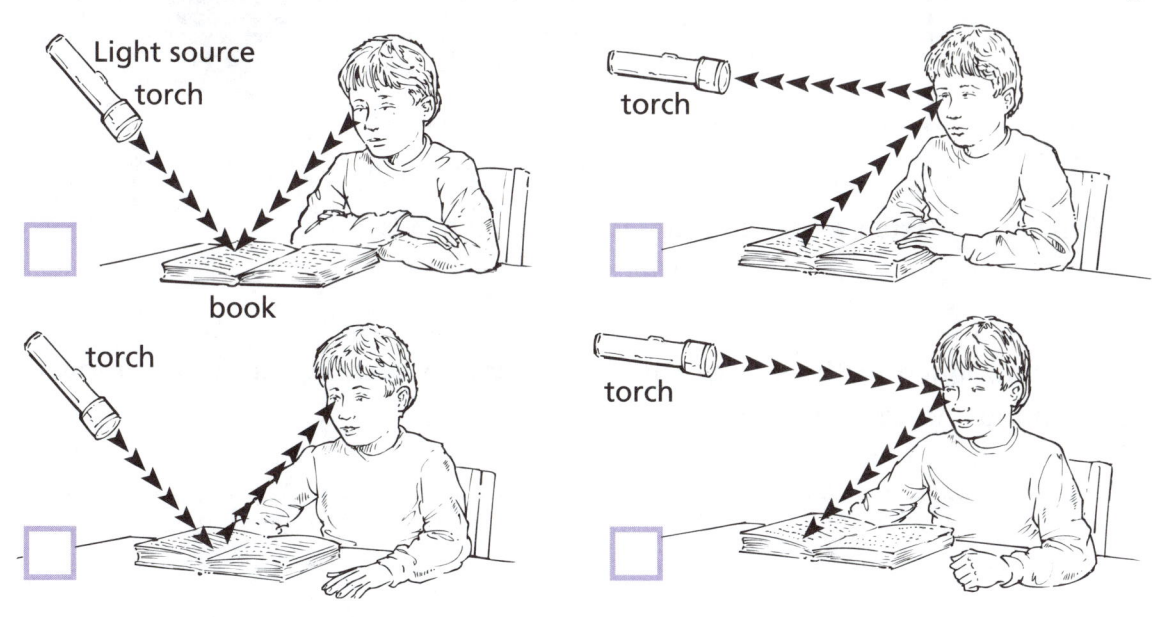

   Light source torch

   book

   torch

   torch

   torch

2. Look at this picture. Draw on the arrows to show how the boy sees the book.

   Remember! Light travels only in straight lines.

29

Shadows

Yasmin and Robert were using their hands to make animal shapes from the shadows.

This graph shows how the size of the shadows changed when they moved their hands away from the light source.

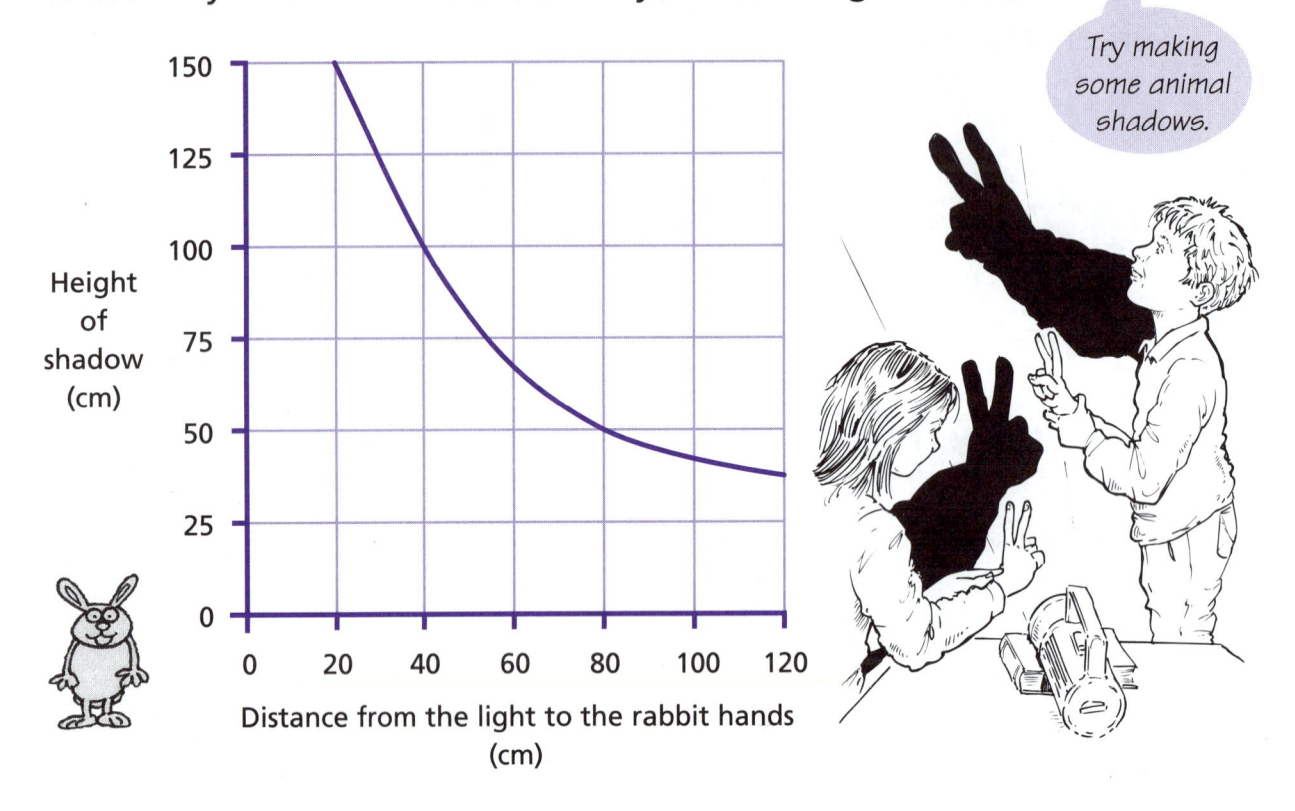

Try making some animal shadows.

Height of shadow (cm)

Distance from the light to the rabbit hands (cm)

1 What happened to the size of the shadow when Yasmin and Robert moved their hands nearer the light?

_____

_____

_____

2 What happened to the size of the shadow when they moved their hands away from the light?

_____

_____

3 At what distance was the shadow 100 cm high? _____

4 What was the height of the shadow when the hands were 80 cm away from the light? _____

30

Reflections

When light rays hit a shiny object they bounce back off it and change direction – this is called **reflection**.

Reflection is like bouncing a ball.

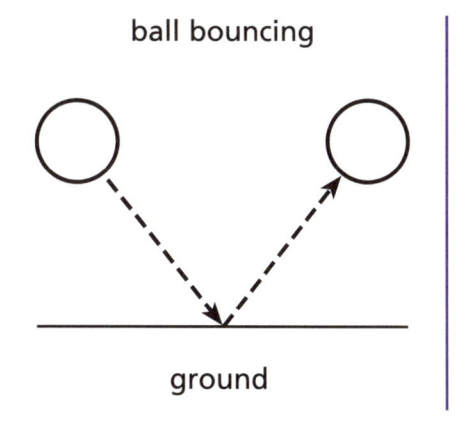

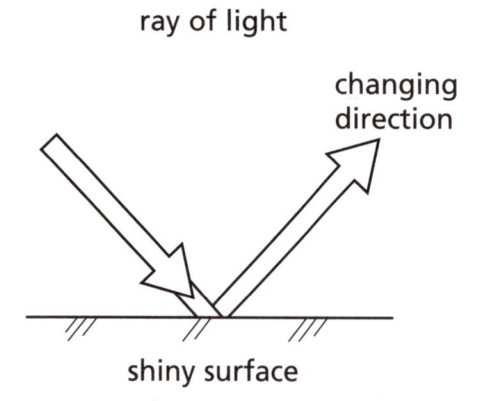

ball bouncing	ray of light
ground	shiny surface

1 Test these objects to see if they reflect the light. Put a ✓ beside each of the objects that reflect light. Put a ✗ beside the objects that don't reflect light.

Object	Does it reflect light?
paper	
metal knife	
foil	
glass	
pencil	
jumper	
book	
apple	
shoe	
mirror	
window	
metal spoon	
wooden spoon	

2 Find two objects of your own to test and write them in the spaces.

3 What do you notice about the objects which reflect the light?

_____

_____

31

Peeping round corners

When light is **reflected** it changes direction when it hits a shiny surface.

Use a mirror to see if you can see round corners.

Use a mirror to see if you can see under the table when you are sitting in a chair at the table.

Submarines have a **periscope** which sailors use to see on the surface of the water when the submarine is under the water.

Satwinda has made a periscope of her own.

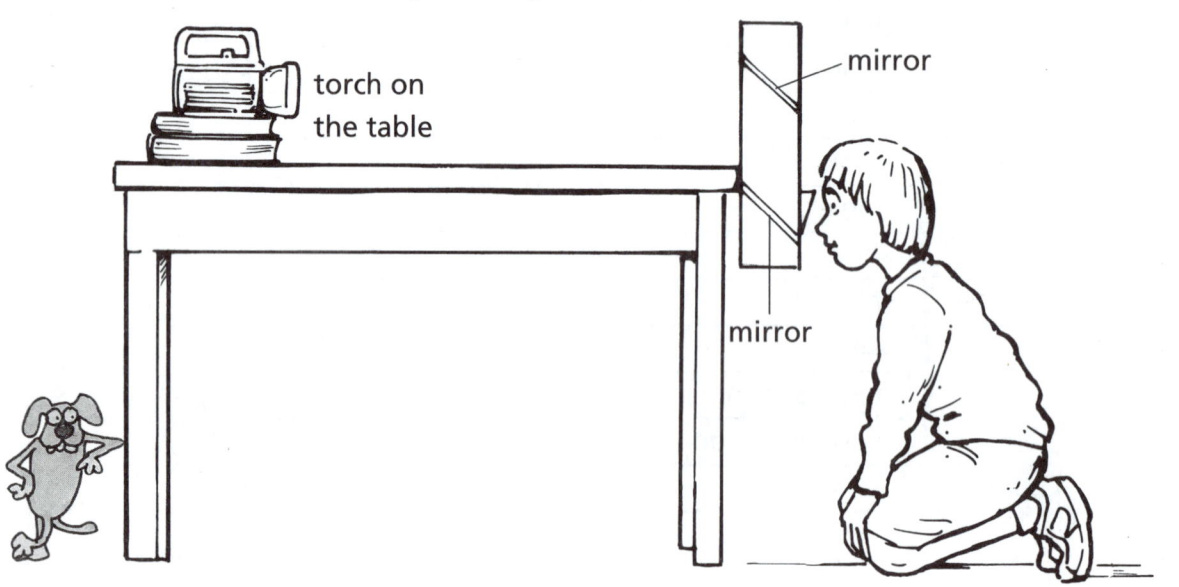

torch on the table

mirror

mirror

1 Draw arrows on the diagram to show how Satwinda can see the torch.

2 Explain how she can see the torch.

_____

_____

True or false?

Do this test to see how much you know about seeing!

3 Read these statements about light, reflection and seeing. Are they true or false? Put a ✓ beside statements that are correct. Put a ✗ beside statements that are false.

(a) The light enters our eyes. ☐

(b) We send out rays from our eyes to see things. ☐

(c) Flat, shiny surfaces reflect light best. ☐

(d) Smaller shadows are made as you move the object further away from the light. ☐

(e) My shadow is made by my reflection. ☐

(f) Shadows are made by transparent objects. ☐

(g) We can see the shadow of an object because light is blocked by the object. ☐

(h) A spoon looks shiny because it gives out light. ☐

(i) Light travels in wavy lines. ☐

(j) If we close our eyes we cannot see the light because it cannot enter our eyes. ☐

(k) When light bounces off a rough surface it is reflected. ☐

4 For the false statements write the correct version here.

_____
_____
_____
_____
_____
_____
_____
_____

33

Dissolving

Some solids **dissolve** in water, others do not.

Look at the substances below. Sort them into two groups: those that dissolve in water and those that don't.

Try them out yourself if you are not sure ... but ask an adult first.

The water should be clear if the substance has dissolved.

cornflour   flour   instant coffee   washing powder   salt

sand   custard powder   tea leaves   icing sugar   jelly

baking powder   sugar   cornflakes   talcum powder   rice

Dissolves in water	Does not dissolve in water

Hot stuff

Does the **temperature** of the water make a difference to how quickly substances **dissolve**?

Harry and Melanie did an investigation to find out. This is a graph to show the dissolving times of sugar in water at various temperatures.

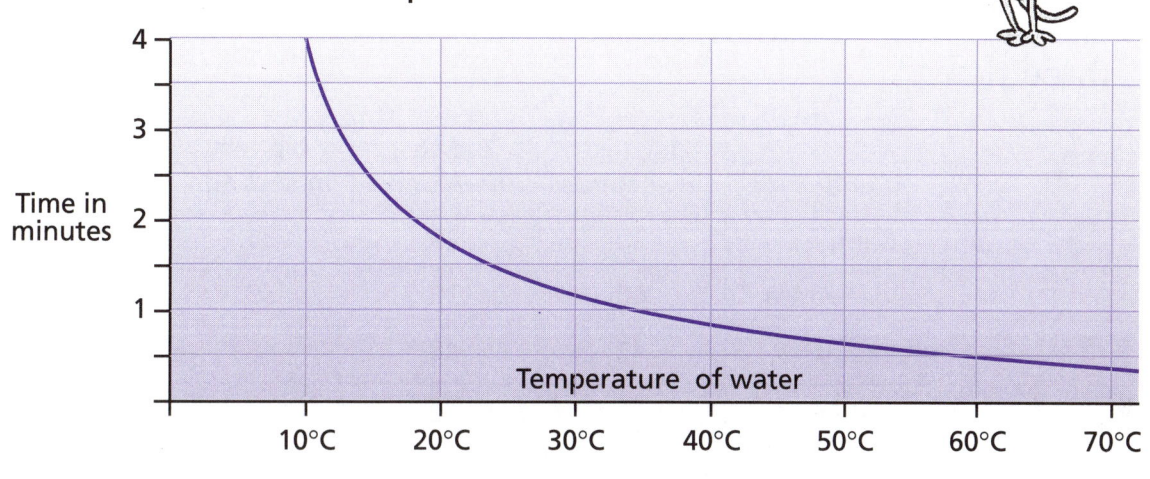

Time in minutes / Temperature of water

1 What does this graph show? _____
_____
_____

Are there any other factors which affect how quickly sugar dissolves? The number of stirs and the amount of water are two more variables that could be investigated.

2 Choose one of these variables to investigate. List the equipment you will need.
_____
_____

3 Plan how you will make it a fair test.
_____
_____

4 What did you find out? _____
_____
_____
_____

Do this with an adult. You can investigate these factors using just cold water from the tap.

Sweet stuff

Will small sugar crystals **dissolve** more quickly than large ones?

Claire carried out an investigation to find out. She **repeated** the test three times.

Sugar type	1st test in seconds	2nd test in seconds	3rd test in seconds
icing	30	29	31
demerara	40	38	39
molasses	47	48	46
white	35	38	38

1 Why did Claire need to repeat the test three times?

_____

2 What would she have to do to make sure the test was fair?

_____

3 Calculate the average time for each type of sugar to dissolve. To calculate the average you find the total number and then divide it by the number of items.

One has been done for you.

icing sugar

30
+29
31
―――
90 ÷ 3 = 30 seconds

demerara sugar

Write your sums here.

molasses

white sugar

You could use a calculator to help you.

36

4 Draw a bar chart to show the average time it took for each sugar to dissolve.

5 What did Claire find out from this investigation?
_____
_____
_____
_____

6 Can you explain this?
_____
_____
_____

Saturation point

Is there a limit to how much of a solid will dissolve in water? Try this investigation to find out.

*When no more salt will dissolve, we say that the solution is **saturated**.*

You will need

- salt
- water
- teaspoon
- plastic measuring jug
- clear plastic container

Ask an adult to help you with this part.

What to do

1. Measure out 10 cm³ of water and pour it into the clear container.
2. Add one teaspoon of salt and stir it in until the salt dissolves.
3. Keep adding spoonfuls of salt but remember to count them.
4. Keep adding salt until no more dissolves into the water.
5. Record your results in the table below.
6. Repeat the experiment again, this time using 20 cm³ of water.
7. Repeat the experiment again, this time using 30 cm³ of water.
8. Repeat the experiment again, this time using 40 cm³ of water.

Results

	10 cm³	20 cm³	30 cm³	40 cm³
Number of spoonfuls				

*When no more of a solid can be dissolved in a liquid, this is called **saturation point**.*

Look carefully at your results.

1 What did you find out from this investigation? _____
_____
_____

2 Is there a pattern in the result? _____

3 How would you describe the pattern? _____
_____

Now try the same experiment using warm water.

Ask an adult to help you with this part.

4 Does the temperature of the water affect how much salt can be dissolved?
_____

Separating mixtures

There are different ways to **separate** materials which do not dissolve in water.

A	B	C
sieve with a wide mesh	sieve with a narrow mesh	filter paper in a funnel

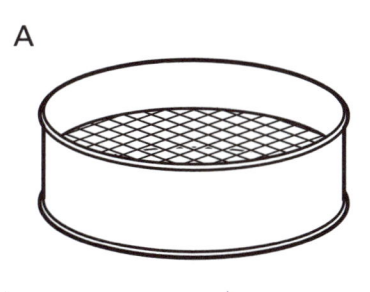

1 Look at the substances on page 34 that did not dissolve. If you wanted to separate them from the water, which method would you use?
Fill in the table.

*Using filter paper to separate mixtures is called **filtration**.*

Substance	Method

Substance	Method

Try making a funnel yourself and filtering one of the substances listed in your table. Cut a plastic drinks bottle in half. Line the bottle with filter paper (used in a coffee machine) or a piece of paper towel.

Ask an adult to help you.

Write out the steps in order and give each one a number.

2 Explain what happens when you put the mixture in the filter. _____

_____

_____

_____

3 Draw a picture of what was left in the filter.

Recovering materials

Ali carried out an investigation using salt. He dissolved some salt into water.
Then he left it for a few days. He found the water had **evaporated** and only salt was left.

Does this happen with any other solids?
Try testing coffee and sugar.

Remember – the water should be clear when the solid has dissolved.

You will need

- 2 identical cups
- 2 identical saucers
- teaspoon
- warm water
- sugar
- coffee

What to do

1 Put a teaspoon of sugar in a cup.
2 Fill up the cup with some warm water.
3 Stir in the sugar until it has dissolved.
4 Now put five teaspoons of the solution on the saucer.
5 Put the saucer on to a windowsill or somewhere in the sun.
6 Now do the same for the coffee. Leave them for a few days.

1 Described what happened. _____

2 Explain why this happened. _____

3 What is this process called?

4 Some solids can be **recovered** after they have been mixed with water, some cannot. Look at the materials in the table. Mark those which you can recover from water with a Y. Mark those you think cannot be recovered from water with an N.

Sugar can be recovered after it has been mixed with water, because you can let the water evaporate, leaving the sugar behind.

water and sand		water and soil	
water and salt		water and chalk	
water and sugar		water and rice	
water and cement		water and talcum	
water and bath salts		water and plaster of Paris	

5 Look again at the table above.
How would you recover the materials marked with a Y?

_____
_____
_____
_____
_____
_____
_____
_____
_____
_____
_____
_____
_____
_____

41

Speed up!

Ali said he could get water to **evaporate more quickly** by using a container with a wide opening.

These are the containers he used.

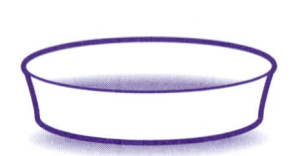

He investigated his prediction to see if he was correct. Here are the results.

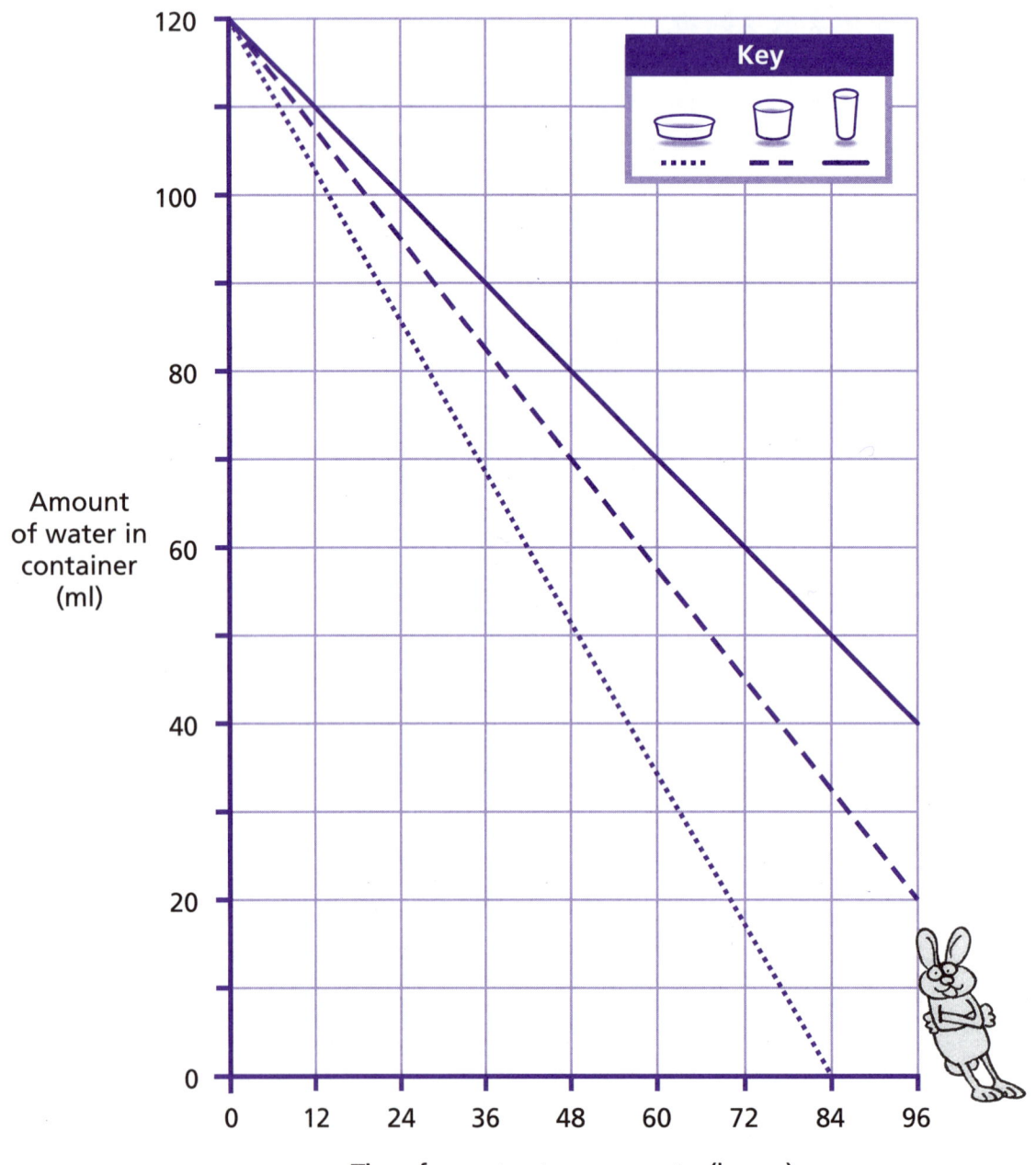

1 What do you observe from the graph?

_____
_____
_____
_____
_____
_____

2 What did Ali need to do to make the test fair?

_____
_____
_____
_____
_____

3 Draw a ring around the container which will allow the water to evaporate quickest.

4 Why did you choose this one?

_____
_____
_____
_____
_____
_____

Change it back

Hannah left a chocolate bar in her bag on a hot day, where it melted. She put it in a fridge to see what would happen.

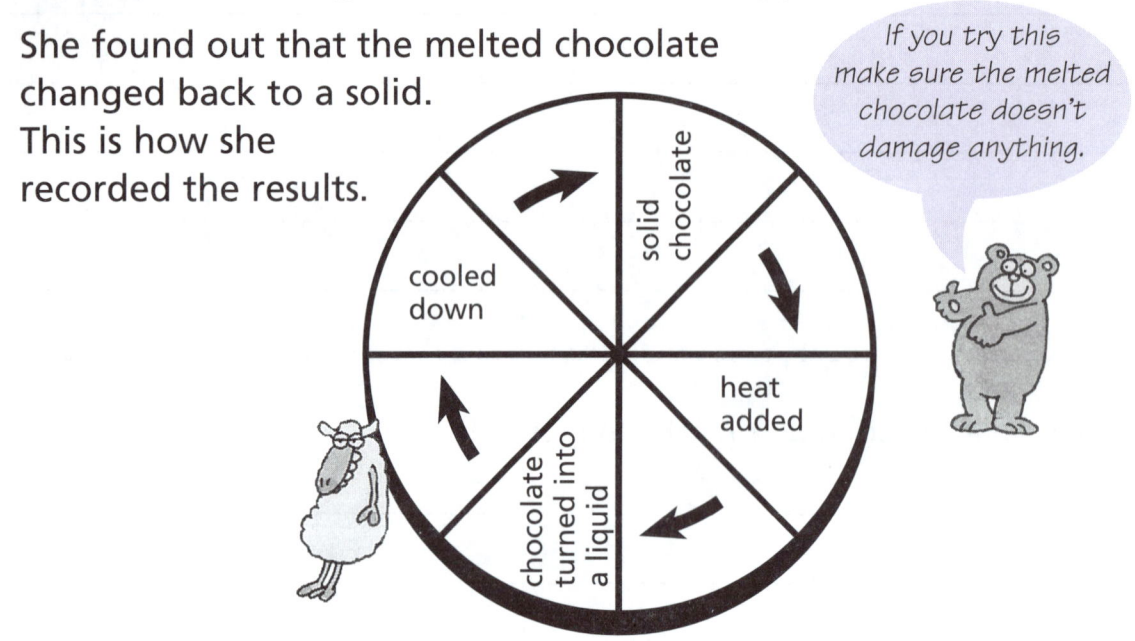

She found out that the melted chocolate changed back to a solid. This is how she recorded the results.

If you try this make sure the melted chocolate doesn't damage anything.

We say that this is a **reversible change** because the chocolate can be changed back to its original state.

Does this happen to all substances?

1 Look at the list of substances and decide which can be changed back to their original state after they have been heated and cooled. Put a tick in the box beside the ones that undergo reversible changes.

ice cubes ☐   eggs ☐   butter ☐   clay ☐   popcorn ☐

2 Draw a diagram like the one above to show the changes for two of the substances.

Choose substances that undergo reversible changes.

44

Reversible or irreversible?

When you can't change a material back to its original state it has undergone an **irreversible change**.

1 Look at the materials in the table below and write down whether the change is reversible or irreversible when they are heated.

Material	Reversible or irreversible change
cake mixture	
raw meat	
potatoes	
chocolate	
water	
butter	
bread slices	
sugar	
ice cream	

2 Think of some materials of your own to add to the table.

If a change is irreversible then a new material has been created.

3 Where an irreversible change has taken place, list the new material that has been created.

Original material	New material created

45

Volcano

Try making your own model **volcano**.

You will need

- newspapers
- baking powder
- plasticene or modelling clay
- small plastic beaker
- vinegar

What to do

1. Cover the table or working area with newspaper.
2. Put some baking powder in the small beaker.
3. Place the beaker in the middle of the newspaper area.
4. Build up the volcano around the beaker using modelling clay.
5. Drip a few drops of vinegar into the mouth of the volcano.
6. Stand back and observe what happens.

Try adding a few drops of red food colouring!

1 Draw a diagram of what happens.

2 Describe what happens. _____

_____

_____

3 Is this a reversible or irreversible change? _____

4 How do you know? _____

_____

_____

_____

Burning

Never burn anything unless an adult is with you.

When something **burns**, you can see a flame.

Look carefully at the picture.

1 Colour in red the places where burning is taking place.

2 Choose three of the burning items and describe what happens to the material.

_____

_____

_____

3 Is burning reversible or irreversible? _____

*When an object burns, two things are given out – **heat** and **gases**.*

Do you know the name of the black substance that forms on something burning?

47

What happens?

Listed below are a number of different processes that can act on materials.

melting   mixing   burning   freezing   baking   condensation   dissolving   evaporation

The first one has been done for you.

1 Look carefully at the different processes and decide which one is taking place in each of the situations below.

Material	Heated or cooled?	Changes	Process	Reversible or irreversible?
water	heated	water disappeared	evaporation	reversible
butter	heated	became runny liquid		
wood	heated	turned black		
salt dissolved in water	heated	salt crystals produced		
steam	cooled	droplets of water produced		
water	cooled	solid blocks produced		
clay	heated	became firm to touch, kept its shape		
chocolate	heated	became runny liquid		
dough	heated	became firm to touch, kept its shape		

2 Think of two more examples to add to the table. Try to include any of the processes that are not already in the table.

Did you find examples of all the processes?

48

Word puzzle

Complete this word puzzle by answering the clues below.

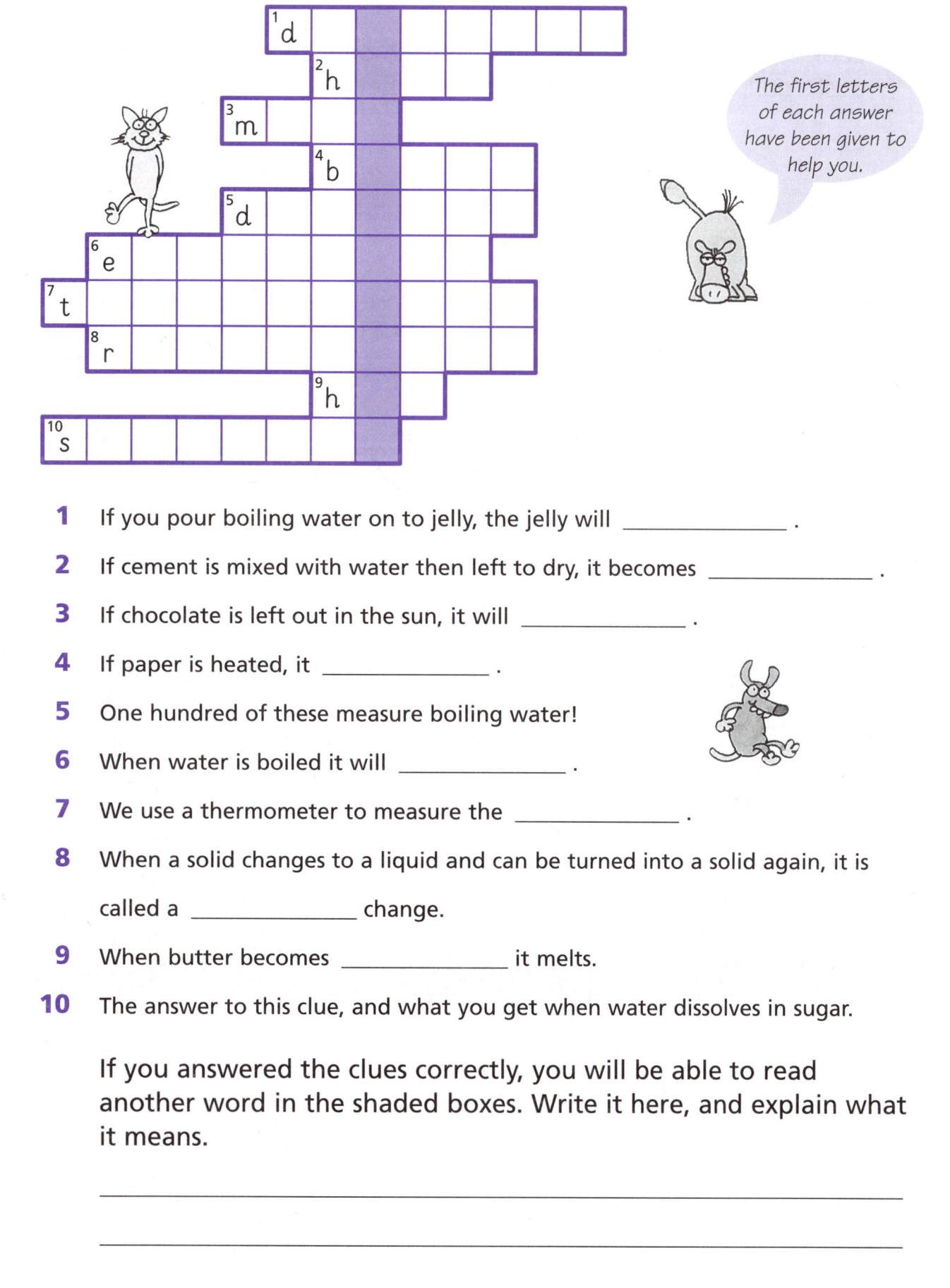

The first letters of each answer have been given to help you.

1 If you pour boiling water on to jelly, the jelly will _____ .

2 If cement is mixed with water then left to dry, it becomes _____ .

3 If chocolate is left out in the sun, it will _____ .

4 If paper is heated, it _____ .

5 One hundred of these measure boiling water!

6 When water is boiled it will _____ .

7 We use a thermometer to measure the _____ .

8 When a solid changes to a liquid and can be turned into a solid again, it is called a _____ change.

9 When butter becomes _____ it melts.

10 The answer to this clue, and what you get when water dissolves in sugar.

If you answered the clues correctly, you will be able to read another word in the shaded boxes. Write it here, and explain what it means.

_____

_____

Forcing it

Forces are pushes, pulls or twists that cause objects to move, stop moving or change direction.

Look at the pictures below and for each one identify whether a push, pull or twist is causing the movement.

A

B

C

D

E

F

G

H

I

J

K

L

Push	Pull	Twist

Write the letter of each picture in the correct column.

50

Forcemeters

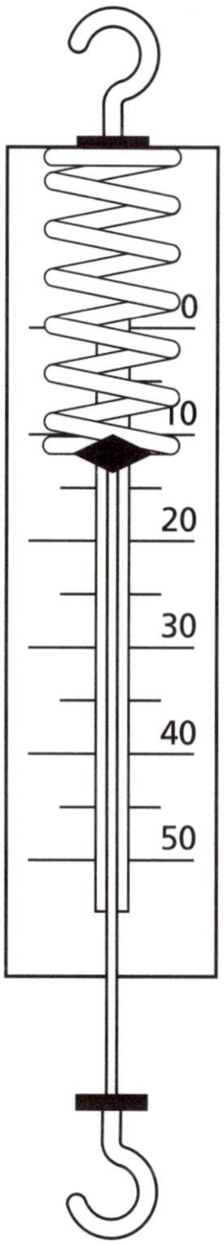

Forcemeters are used to measure force.

Forces are measured in Newtons.

1. Look at the picture of a forcemeter.
   Colour in the spring.

2. Why do you think a forcemeter needs a spring?
   Tick the correct answers.

   because it's strong ☐   because it's metal ☐

   because it's stretchy ☐   because it's shiny ☐

   We write Newtons as N.

   For example, we write 6 Newtons as 6N.

3. Look carefully at these different forcemeters.
   Read the amount of force measured on each one.
   Write the amount in the box underneath each picture.

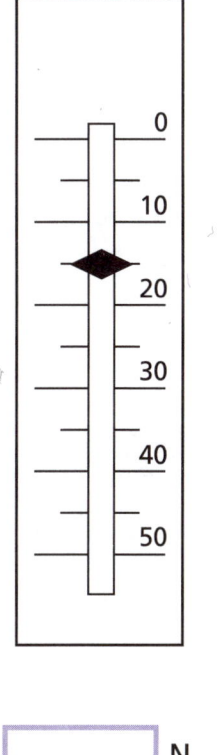

   (a) ☐ N 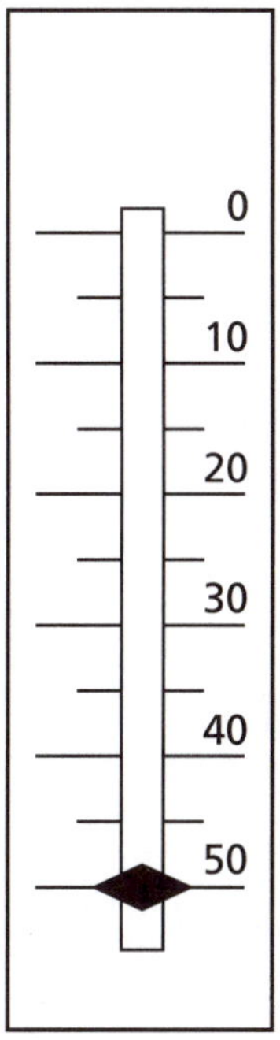   (b) ☐ N 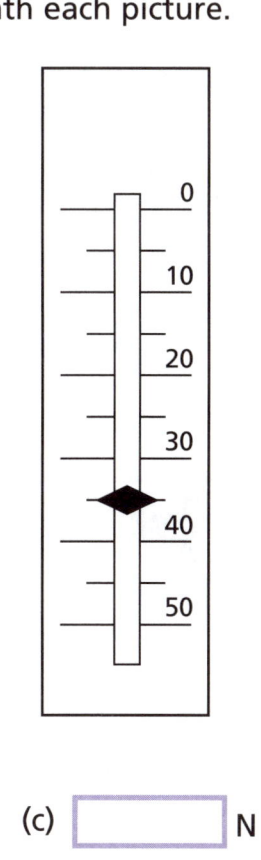   (c) ☐ N   (d) ☐ N

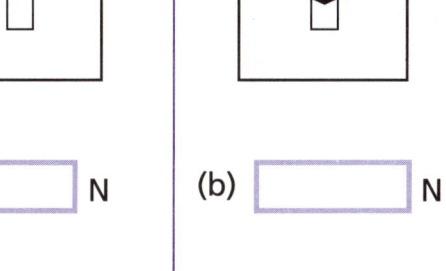

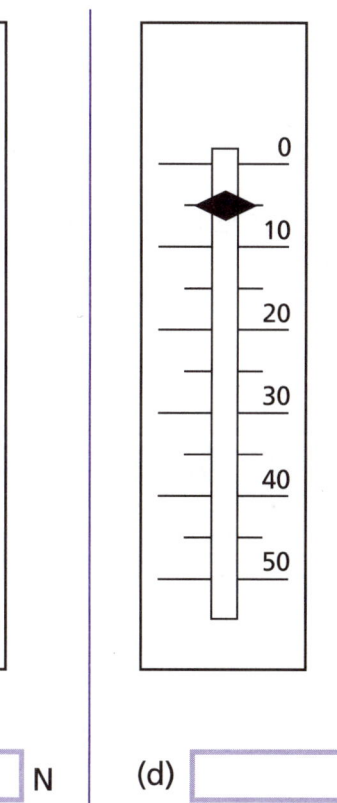

51

Gravity

If we drop an object it falls to the ground because of the Earth's **gravitational pull**.

Objects have a weight because **gravity** pulls on them. The greater the pull of gravity the greater the weight.

1 Make a weighing machine.

You will need

- a hook or somewhere to attach an elastic band (e.g. door handle)
- long elastic band
- yoghurt pot
- sticky tape
- ruler or measuring tape
- string

What to do

1. Attach the string to the yoghurt pot using the sticky tape.
2. Tie the string to the elastic band.
3. Loop the other end of the elastic band over a hook or door handle.
4. Make a collection of small objects such as pens, a rubber, stones, teaspoon, coins, marbles, etc.
5. Put each object into the yoghurt pot, one at a time.
6. Measure the length of the elastic band each time.

2 Record the length in the table.

Object	Length of elastic band (mm)

3 Now plot your results on a bar chart.

What measurements will you have here?

Write the names of the objects here.

4 What do your results tell you?

_____

_____

_____

_____

5 Try to find out how other weighing machines (e.g. bathroom scales or kitchen scales) work.

Air resistance

Air resistance is the force that slows objects down as they fall through the air.

James tested this using two pieces of paper. He screwed up one piece into a ball and kept the other piece flat.
He dropped the two pieces at the same time from the same height. The ball fell much quicker than the flat piece.

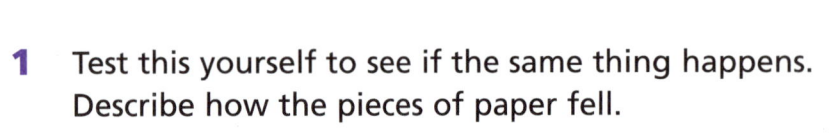

1 Test this yourself to see if the same thing happens. Describe how the pieces of paper fell.

	How paper fell
flat piece of paper	
ball of paper	

Why do you think this happened? _____
_____

2 Look at these pictures of parachutes and decide which one would be best at slowing down the person. _____

A

B

C

D

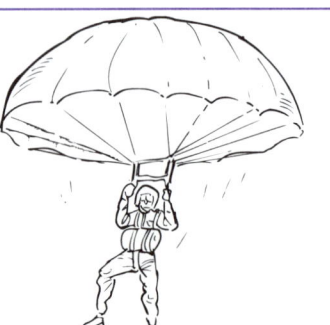

3 Put the parachutes in order starting with the slowest. ☐ ☐ ☐ ☐

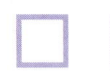

Streamlined

Air resistance slows objects down that fall to the ground, but it also slows objects as they move through the air.

Look at the pictures of different types of transport. Some are **streamlined** so that they are not slowed down so much by the air resistance.

Tick the pictures where the objects are streamlined.

Spinners

What affects the speed of a spinner falling through the air?

To find out, make a spinner by following these instructions. Ask an adult to help you with the cutting.

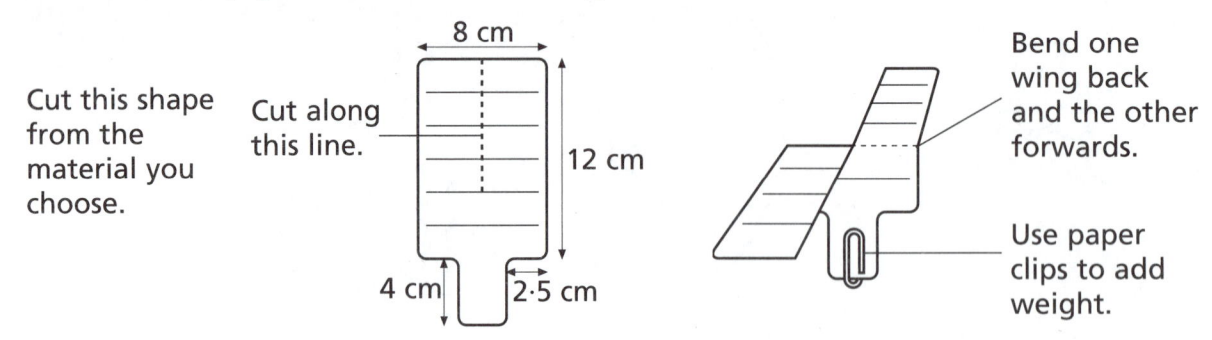

Cut this shape from the material you choose.

Cut along this line.

8 cm

12 cm

4 cm   2·5 cm

Bend one wing back and the other forwards.

Use paper clips to add weight.

Investigate one of these variables:
- the length of the wing of the spinner
- the type of paper used for the spinner
- the weight of the spinner.

1 Use this chart to design a fair test to find out the answer.

This depends on which variable you have chosen to investigate.

| What I want to find out. |
| What I will use. |
| What I will do. |
| How I will make the test fair. |
| How I will record my observations. |

*Write about it **and** draw a diagram.*

2 What do you predict will happen in the test?

_____

_____

3 Describe what you did.

_____
_____
_____
_____
_____
_____

4 Did you have to change your plans? _____

5 Why? _____
_____
_____

6 Record your results in a table.

This is your conclusion.

7 What did you find out from your investigation? _____
_____
_____

8 Were there any patterns or trends in your results? _____
_____
_____

9 Were your results the same as your prediction?
_____

All change

Forces can make objects speed up, slow down, start and stop moving and **change direction**.

Listed below are different types of forces.

Match the force with the correct definition.

Draw a line to join the word and its definition.

upthrust	A force that acts between two solid surfaces when they come into contact and slows the moving objects down.
magnetism	A force that makes things fall and that acts on you and everything else on Earth all the time.
air resistance	A force that acts on objects that are in the water and pushes them up.
friction	A force that acts on objects going through the air and slows moving objects down.
gravity	A force that acts on two pieces of iron or steel causing them to attract or repel each other.

Tug o' war

When objects are stationary the two forces acting in opposite directions are **balanced**. One force is not stronger than the other, so they are **equal**.

It is like a tug of war game.

If the forces pulling on the rope in opposite directions are equal then neither team will win.

Team A   Team B

1 What happens to the rope if the two sides are of the same (or equal) strength?

_____

_____

Team A   Team B

2 In this game, Team B is moving backwards.

Why? _____

_____

_____

Team A   Team B

Explain your answers by describing what has happened to the forces each time.

3 In this game, Team A is moving backwards.

Why? _____

_____

_____

Drawing arrows

There is usually more than one force acting on an object, even if you think there is only one. One of the forces may be stronger than the other(s).

In these pictures the arrows have been drawn in to represent the forces acting.

The direction of the arrow shows the **direction of the force**.
The length of the arrow shows the **strength of the force**.

1   Write the names of the forces in the boxes on each picture.

2   Underneath each picture write which force is the strongest.

Look back at the definitions on page 58 to help you.

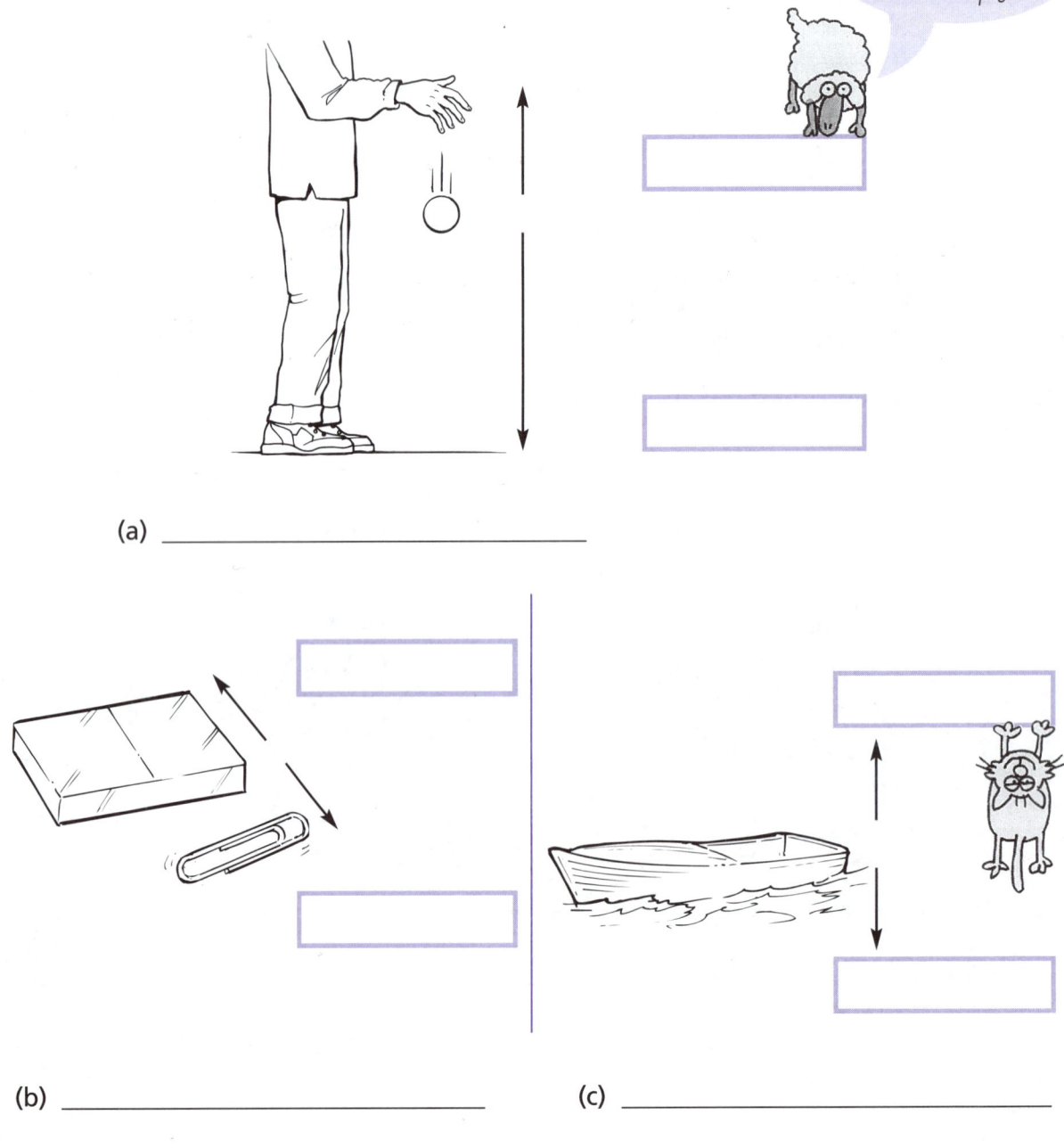

(a) _____

(b) _____   (c) _____

3 In the pictures below, the arrows haven't been drawn in. That's your job.

Remember – the length of the arrow shows the strength of the force.

The direction of the arrow shows the direction of the force.

Explain what's happening to the forces in each picture.

(a) _____

(b) _____

(c) _____

(d) _____

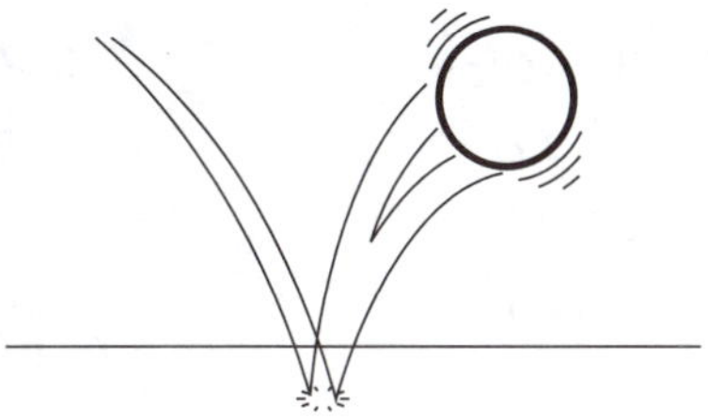

Draw one of your own here.

(e) _____

(f) _____

61

Puzzler

Start with the longest words!

Fill in the spaces using the words listed below.

i
r
r
e
v
e
r
s
i
b
l
e

4 letter words
germ
prey

5 letter words
mould

6 letter words
change
mirror
newton
opaque
weight

7 letter words
balance
circuit
gravity
habitat
microbe
mixture
reflect

8 letter words
bacteria
condense
consumer
predator
producer
solution
upthrust

9 letter words
component
conductor
dissolved
evaporate
insulator
nutrients

10 letter words
fertiliser
forcemeter
reversible
stationary

Answers and Hints

In some instances there may be more than one possible answer so you may need to check that the answer your child has given is reasonable. As long as your child's answer makes sense and has shown they understand the question, you should mark it right. Sometimes the question will ask them to express an opinion, to make a prediction or to create their own piece of work. When marking your child's efforts please remember that encouragement is always more helpful than criticism.

PAGE 5
1 D   **2** C   **3** G   **4** A   **5** B   **6** F   **7** E

PAGES 6 & 7
1 (Fruit) tomato, cucumber, apple, lemon, orange, mango, walnuts; (Leaves) spinach, lettuce, cabbage, tea; (Seeds) sunflower seeds, corn, peas, beans; (Stem) rhubarb, celery, bean sprouts; (Roots) swede, parsnip, carrot, potato, radish, beetroots; (Flower) cauliflower   **2** Check that the foods your child has chosen have been written in the correct boxes.

PAGES 8 & 9
1 plant 5   **2** it has all the correct conditions (light, water, heat and fertiliser)   **3** in a cupboard   **4** it had no light but was still warm (it was inside)   **5** in an open-top ice box (for instance, a wooden box containing ice with a top layer of sawdust to keep the ice cool)   **6** it had light but was kept cold   **7** light, water, heat and nutrients (fertiliser)   **8** (a) 1, (b) 5, (c) 2, (d) 4, (e) 3

PAGE 10
correct numbers in boxes: (a) 3, (b) 4, (c) 1, (d) 5, (e) 6, (f) 2

PAGE 11
correct names: (tufted vetch) C, (hedge-parsley) A, (foxglove) E, (campion) B, (white deadnettle) F, (herb Robert) D

PAGES 12 & 13
1 (Zone A) long beaks for catching fish, webbed feet for moving in water, long wings for gliding above the water; (Zone B) birds are smaller for moving through trees and branches, smaller beaks for catching insects and eating seeds and berries; (Zone C) long legs for wading, long beaks to catch fish in shallow water or creatures living in mud   **2** Check that your child has found some sensible names (possible answers (Zone A) puffins, ospreys, gannets, cormorants (Zone B) blackbirds, pigeons, thrushes, woodpeckers (Zone C) kingfishers, herons, moorhens, geese

PAGE 14
connected plants and boxes: Seaweed–lives in salty and rocky seashores–has gas-filled bubbles...; Foxglove–lives in shady areas–likes damp conditions...; Marram grass–lives in sandy areas–has very long roots...; Water lily–lives in fresh water–has long leaf stalks...; Cactus–lives in desert areas–water is stored in the fleshy parts...

PAGES 15
1 sand   **2** has large particles, water passes easily through the gaps   **3** clay   **4** has small particles, the gaps are very small so water can only drain through very slowly   **5** loam   **6** has a mixture of particle sizes, so there are big and small gaps and water passes through gradually   **7** loam   **8** water drains slowly, so will not be too dry or too wet

PAGES 16 & 17
1 no – consumers eat other things instead of making their own food   **2** (correct order) wheat–mouse–owl   **3** grass–zebra–lion   **4** plankton–pilchard–tuna–human   **5** seaweed–winkle– crab–seagull   **6** leaf–caterpillar–robin–hawk   **7** shrub–insect–frog–grass snake   **8** (Producers) grass, wheat, plankton, seaweed, leaf, shrub; (Consumers which eat producers) rabbit, winkle, mouse, zebra, pilchard, caterpillar, insect; (Consumers which eat consumers) fox, frog, crab, owl, lion, tuna, human, seagull, robin, hawk, grass snake   **9** producers always come first – only producers make their own food; consumers can only survive by feeding off producers (or other consumers who have already fed off producers)

PAGE 18
1 tin–C, plastic bag–C, bottle–C, cardboard box–B, mug–C, newspaper–A, coins–C, leaves–A, nail–C, vegetable peelings–A, twigs–B, glass–C, nappy–B, brick–C, plastic cup–C, hamburger carton–C, dead animal–A, crisp packet–C, chewing gum–B, car tyre–C   **2** micro-organisms break down the rubbish   **3** a lot of rubbish will not be broken down by micro-organisms so it will stay around for hundreds of years; we should try not to pollute the land; in the future we will run out of places to bury rubbish

PAGE 19
1 (Caused by micro-organisms) measles, a cold, 'flu, chicken pox, mumps, German measles, stomach bug, meningitis; (Not caused by micro-organisms) broken arm, splinter, nose bleed, bruise, bad eyesight   **2** (ways germs are transmitted) sneezing without covering your mouth, letting other people use your handkerchief

PAGE 20
1 round the base of the teeth, along the gums   **2** small particles of food are trapped between the teeth and along the gums and are only removed if teeth are cleaned properly after a meal   **3** brush my teeth properly after meals to get rid of food particles on my teeth   **4** clean your teeth properly, don't eat so many sugary things, and always chew your food properly to help keep teeth strong and your gums healthy

PAGE 21
1 ensure that the container and the balloon are the same size each time; add the same amount of water to each container; use the same amount of yeast; wait the same length of time; keep the bottles in the same place at the same temperature   **2** the balloons inflated by different amounts; nothing happened to the balloon over the container with no sugar in it   **3** the balloon on the container with the most sugar inflated the most; yeast grows more if it has more sugar   **4** the gas given off makes the bread rise

PAGE 22
1 (a) Slice 4, (b) Slice 2, (c) Slice 1, (d) Slice 3   **2** make sure all the bags are clean, take all the slices of bread from the same loaf of bread, keep the bags in the same place (and for the same amount of time)

PAGE 23
1 (connected foods and explanations) Baked beans–Food is cooked..., Peas–Food is cooled..., Pasta–Water is removed...   **2** (freezing) water and air, but no warmth; (canning) warmth and water, but no air; (drying) warmth and air, but no water

PAGES 24 & 25
1 Check that your child has coloured circuits A and D (they are complete)   **2** circuit B won't light because the wire is not connected to the battery; circuit C won't light because the paper clip 'switch' is open   **3** so that electricians/electrical engineers will be able to understand plans (and that children doing experiments can too!)   **4** electrical engineers   **5** (a) B, (b) D, (c) A, (d) C   **6** (a) bulb, switch (paper clip), motor, three batteries, wires; (b) four bulbs, switch, three batteries, wires; (c) two motors, two batteries, bulb, switch, wires; (d) three bulbs, switch, motor, two batteries, wires

PAGES 26 & 27
1 (ticked items) fewer bulbs, thicker wire, shorter wire, bigger battery   **2** (a) right-hand circuit is brighter because there are fewer bulbs; (b) left-hand circuit is brighter because it has more batteries; (c) right-hand circuit is brighter because there is less wire in the circuit   **3** the longer the wire the less bright the bulb is (there is more wire for the electricity to pass through and so less electricity goes through the bulb)   **4** they used the same type of bulb, same type of battery, and the same thickness wire for all tests   **5** (a) true, (b) true, (c) false, (d) false

PAGE 28
1 both bulbs will go out; opening the switch breaks the whole circuit and no current flows through the bulbs   **2** only one bulb will go out; opening one switch breaks only one branch of the circuit, and current can still flow through the other bulb   **3** parallel (there can be one switch for every bulb)

PAGE 29
1 only the bottom left picture is correct   **2** Your child should have drawn arrows from the window to the book, and then from the book to the boy's eyes. Check that the arrows are pointing in the right direction (window to book, book to eye).

PAGE 30
1 the shadows got bigger   **2** the shadows got smaller   **3** 40 cm   **4** 50 cm

PAGE 31
1 (objects which reflect light) metal knife, foil, glass, mirror, window, metal spoon   **2** Check that your child has written two other objects into the space in the chart, and has correctly said whether or not they reflect light.   **3** they are made of metal and glass

PAGES 32 & 33
1 Your child should have drawn arrows from the torch to the top mirror, then down from the top mirror to the bottom mirror, and then into the child's eye. Check that they have drawn the arrows in the right direction (from torch to eyes, via the mirrors).   **2** the torch light reflects off the top mirror, then reflects off the bottom mirror, and then reaches Satwinda's eyes   **3** (a) true, (b) false, (c) true, (d) true, (e) false, (f) false, (g) true, (h) false, (i) false, (j) true, (k) false   **4** (true versions, in order) A light source sends out rays of light which go into our eyes. My shadow is made because my body blocks the light. Transparent objects do not make a shadow because light passes through them. A spoon looks shiny because it reflects light well. Light travels in straight lines. Light only reflects off smooth surfaces.

PAGE 34
(dissolves in water) washing powder, instant coffee, salt, icing sugar, jelly, baking powder, sugar; (does not dissolve in water) cornflour, flour, sand, custard powder, tea leaves, cornflakes, talcum powder, rice.   Check that your child understands that something only properly dissolves in water if the water goes clear afterwards.

PAGE 35
1 sugar dissolves more quickly in hotter water   **2** For both experiments your child would need a clear container (like a glass), water and sugar. To check whether stirring affects how quickly sugar dissolves your child would also need something to stir the water with, such as a spoon.   **3** Check that your child understands what is meant by a 'fair test'. In a fair test only one of the amounts/times/actions involved in a test is changed (and all the others are kept the same).   **4** Your child should have found that sugar will dissolve more quickly if more water is used and if the mixture is stirred.

PAGES 36 & 37
1 Your child should understand that experiments are often repeated several times to allow average results to be calculated. This process can remove the effects of any small changes in the results due to human error, slightly inaccurate measuring of amounts, small variations in room temperature (and other 'environmental' factors).   **2** always use the same amount of water and sugar, always stir the water the same amount, always use water at the same temperature   **3** (demerara sugar) 39 seconds; (molasses)

63

47 seconds; (white sugar) 37 seconds   **4** Check that your child has drawn a bar chart correctly. The vertical axis should measure the time taken for the sugar to dissolve (and go up to 50 seconds), and the horizontal axis should list the types of sugar. The four bars (one for each sugar) should be drawn at heights representing the number of seconds each took to dissolve, as measured on the vertical axis.   **5** she found that the smaller sugar crystals dissolved the quickest   **6** sugar crystals dissolve from the outside, this means that smaller particles will completely dissolve more quickly than larger particles

PAGE 38
1 more salt dissolves in more water   **2 & 3** Can your child see a pattern? The amount of salt dissolved goes up when more water is used, but your child should see that the number of spoonfuls of sugar increase roughly in proportion to the amount of water used (although their results may not show this precise pattern very clearly).   **4** yes, more salt can dissolve in the same amount of water if the water is hotter

PAGE 39
1 (Check that your child has copied out the correct eight substances from page 34) cornflour–C, flour–C, sand–C, custard powder–C, pasta–B or C, cornflakes–A, B or C, talcum powder–C, rice–B or C   **2** the water drained through the filter and the substance was left on the filter paper   **3** Check your child's drawing.

PAGES 40 & 41
1 the water disappeared and solid coffee and sugar was left in the bottom of the saucer   **2** the Sun's heat evaporated the water from the saucer, leaving the solid particles behind   **3** evaporation   **4** (first column) Y, Y, N, Y; (second column) Y, Y, Y, N   **5** (water and sand, water and soil, water and chalk, water and rice, water and talcum) use a funnel and filter paper; (water and salt, water and sugar, water and bath salts) evaporate the water by placing the mixture in sunlight, or put in a pan on a cooker and apply a little heat

PAGES 42 & 43
1 the graph shows that water does evaporate more quickly from a container with a wider opening   **2** ensure that each container contains the same amount of water and is kept in the same conditions   **3** the third container would allow the water to evaporate fastest   **4** the exposed surface area of the water is greatest in this container (in the first container the surface area starts big but reduces as the water evaporates; the opposite is true in the second container)

PAGE 44
1 (ticked substances) ice cubes, butter   **2** (ice cubes) ice–heat added–ice turned to water–cooled down; (butter) butter–heat added–butter turned soft/melted–cooled down

PAGE 45
1 (cake mixture) irreversible; (raw meat) irreversible; (potatoes) irreversible; (chocolate) reversible; (water) reversible; (butter) reversible; (bread slices) irreversible; (sugar) irreversible; (ice cream) reversible   **2** Check the substances that your child has added to the table – have they correctly identified them as reversible or irreversible?   **3** (original material and new material) cake mixture–cake; raw meat–cooked meat; potatoes–cooked potatoes; bread slices–toast; sugar–caramel

PAGE 46
1 Check your child's drawing.   **2** the baking powder and vinegar bubble up and runs down the outside of the model volcano   **3** irreversible   **4** the baking powder and vinegar have changed into another substance (and you cannot recover the baking powder)

PAGE 47
1 Your child should have coloured the candles (five of them), the barbecue, the bonfire and the Sun (they might have missed the last one – if so, ask them to think about the question again and look carefully at the picture).   **2** (candle) the candle wax is burnt and slowly used up; (barbecue) the charcoal or wood is burnt and turns to ash; (bonfire) the wood is burnt and turns to ash; (Sun) the Sun is a big ball made of millions and millions of 'atoms'; these atoms smash into each other and make bigger 'particles'; when this happens they release heat and light   **3** irreversible

PAGE 48
1 (butter) melting, reversible; (wood) burning, irreversible; (salt dissolved in water) evaporation, reversible; (steam) condensation, reversible; (water) freezing, reversible; (clay) baking, irreversible; (chocolate) melting, reversible; (dough) baking, irreversible   **2** Check that your child has thought up two extra answers.

PAGE 49
1 dissolve   **2** hard   **3** melt   **4** burns   **5** degrees   **6** evaporate   **7** temperature   **8** reversible   **9** hot   **10** solution   saturation – this is the process of dissolving a solid (like sugar) into a liquid (like water) until no more solid can be dissolved (the sugar solution is said to be saturated)

PAGE 50
push: E, G, I, K, L   pull: B, C, D, F, H   twist: A, J

PAGE 51
1 Check that your child has correctly coloured in the spring.   **2** (ticked answers) because it's strong, because it's stretchy   **3** (left to right) 15, 50, 35, 5

PAGES 52 & 53
2 Check that your child has filled in the chart correctly, recording the length of the elastic band for several different objects.   **3** Check that your child has drawn a bar chart correctly. The vertical axis should measure the length of the elastic band, and the horizontal axis should list the objects used. The bars (one for each object) should be drawn at heights representing the length of the elastic band, as measured on the vertical axis.   **4** the different lengths of the elastic band show how heavy the different objects are; heavier objects are pulled down more by gravity and this extends the elastic band

PAGE 54
1 (flat piece of paper) fell slowly, from side to side; (ball of paper) fell quickly, straight down; (why?) the flat piece of paper has more surface area than the ball of paper and so is slowed down more by air resistance   **2** D   **3** D, A, B, C

PAGE 55
ticked vehicles: racing car, motorbike, saloon car, space rocket, jet plane, propeller plane

PAGES 56 & 57
1 (What I want to find out) What affects how fast a spinner falls through the air.; (What I will use) A spinner made out of paper and a paperclip.; (What I will do) I will drop the spinner and use a watch with a second hand to measure how long it takes to fall to the ground. I will do the experiment several times changing the length of the wings or the paper or the weight (by adding more paper clips).; (How will I make the test fair) I will always drop the spinner from the same height.; (How will I record my observations) In a table.   **2** Your child should be able to predict that the spinner will fall faster if the wings are smaller and if it is made heavier (by adding more paper clips), but saying how the type of paper affects the speed is more difficult (thicker paper would be heavier, but would also make the wings stiffer, so predicting whether the spinner will speed up or slow down is not obvious).   **3, 4, 5 & 6** Check your child's description matches what they did in the experiment. If they had to change their plans talk about what the problem was and how they fixed it. Check that they have written a table of their results clearly.   **7, 8 & 9** It is important that your child analyses their results carefully – what did they find out? did they see any trends? what was the effect of changing the type of paper used?

PAGE 58
connected words and definitions: upthrust–A force that acts on objects that are in water…; magnetism–A force that acts on two pieces of iron or steel…; air resistance–A force that acts on objects going through the air…; friction–A force that acts between two solid surfaces…; gravity–A force that makes things fall…

PAGE 59
1 the rope doesn't move   **2** Team B is pulling harder than Team A. This means that the force (the pull) on their end of the rope is more than the force on the other end, so the rope moves towards Team B.   **3** Check that your child has correctly described the exact opposite of answer 2.

PAGES 60 & 61
1 & 2 (a) (forces) air resistance and gravity, gravity is stronger; (b) magnetism and magnetism, the two forces are exactly the same (the forces are the same, but only the paper clip moves – check that your child understands that this is because the magnet is heavier not because the force acting on the magnet is any less); (c) upthrust (buoyancy/'floating') and gravity, forces are equal   **3** In each example the moving object (the ball, the car, the rocket, etc.) is being acted on by two forces, one acting in the direction it is moving and another (often gravity) which is acting to slow it down (often in the opposite direction). Check that your child has drawn two arrows and understands what two forces are acting in each case. (a) the kick pushes the ball up and to the right, gravity pulls the ball straight down, (b) the engine of the car pushes forward, air resistance acts on the parachute in the opposite direction to slow the car down, (c) the rocket's engines push the rocket straight up, gravity pulls the rocket straight down, (d) the woman pushes the trolley forward, friction (wheels on floor) pushes against this in the opposite direction, (e) the ball is pushed up and to the right by the floor, gravity pulls it straight down (f) Check your child's example – have they drawn a moving object being acted on by two forces?

PAGE 62

[crossword grid with answers: solution, consumer, germ, prey, producer, habitat, conductor, forcemeter, nutrients, mould, fertiliser, condense, bacteria, reflect, opaque, weight, change]

64